# Great Writers & the Cats who Owned Them

# Great Writers & the Cats who Owned Them

SUSANNAH FULLERTON

BODLEIAN
LIBRARY
PUBLISHING

For Gabrielle –
So many walks, so many talks about books and cats.
Thank you!

First published in 2025 by Bodleian Library Publishing
Broad Street, Oxford OX1 3BG
www.bodleianshop.co.uk

ISBN 978 1 85124 654 0

Text © Susannah Fullerton, 2025
Illustrations © Susie Foster, 2025
This edition © Bodleian Library Publishing, University of Oxford, 2025

Susannah Fullerton has asserted her right to be
identified as the author of this Work.

All rights reserved.

No part of this book may be reproduced, stored in a retrieval
system, or transmitted in any form or by any means, electronic,
mechanical, photocopying, recording, or otherwise, without
the written permission of the Bodleian Library, except for the
purpose of research or private study, or criticism or review.

Publisher: Samuel Fanous
Managing Editor: Susie Foster
Editor: Janet Phillips
Picture Editor: Leanda Shrimpton
Cover design by Dot Little at the Bodleian Library
Designed and typeset by Lucy Morton of illuminati in 11½ on 15 Fournier
Printed and bound in China by C&C Offset Printing Co., Ltd
on 115 gsm Yulong Cream paper

British Library Catalogue in Publishing Data
A CIP record of this publication is available from the British Library

# CONTENTS

| | |
|---|---:|
| INTRODUCTION | 1 |
| HODGE, for whom Dr Johnson bought oysters | 9 |
| *PAWS FOR THOUGHT* Petrarch's cat 22 | |
| SELIMA, whose death was memorialized for Horace Walpole | 24 |
| *PAWS FOR THOUGHT* The mad poet's cat 37 | |
| RUMPELSTILZCHEN, ruler of Robert Southey's 'Cat's Eden' | 39 |
| *PAWS FOR THOUGHT* The literary origins of the Tom cat 52 | |
| MYSOUFF I, who permitted Alexandre Dumas to escort him home | 54 |
| *PAWS FOR THOUGHT* An author and the cat flap 60 | |
| FOSS, who owned Edward Lear | 62 |
| *PAWS FOR THOUGHT* The first book of cat care 74 | |
| BOB, who helped Charles Dickens open letters | 76 |
| *PAWS FOR THOUGHT* The literary Cheshire cat 85 | |
| BAMBINO, whose slave was Mark Twain | 88 |
| *PAWS FOR THOUGHT* The literary hotel cat 100 | |
| LA CHATTE, who held Colette under her spell | 102 |
| *PAWS FOR THOUGHT* The cat of The Incredible Journey 111 | |
| DAFFY, who knew Anne of Green Gables before anybody else | 113 |

PAWS FOR THOUGHT *Kipling's cat* 127

NELSON, who was Chief Mouser to Sir Winston Churchill — 129
PAWS FOR THOUGHT *Library cats* 139

BOISE, who was a Christmas treat for Ernest Hemingway — 142
PAWS FOR THOUGHT *The literary cats of Harry Potter* 156

OLD TIMER, who gained Margaret Mitchell's sympathies — 158
PAWS FOR THOUGHT *Theatre cats* 171

BLITZ, who murdered mice for Dorothy L. Sayers — 173
PAWS FOR THOUGHT *T.S. Eliot's cat poems* 190

SAMBO, who helped Paul Gallico remain in a state of delusion — 192
PAWS FOR THOUGHT *Nursery-rhyme cats* 202

BLUEBELL, who critiqued Dame Muriel Spark's manuscripts — 204
PAWS FOR THOUGHT *The cat who helped children learn to read* 217

EL MAGNIFICO, who enchanted Doris Lessing — 219
PAWS FOR THOUGHT *Socks, the letter-writing cat* 229

WOOSKIT, who morphed into Slinky Malinki for Dame Lynley Dodd — 231

TAILPIECE — 243
NOTES — 248
FURTHER READING — 262
ACKNOWLEDGEMENTS — 267
INDEX — 269

# INTRODUCTION

All was quiet in Reichenau Abbey in Germany. The candle flickered, the Irish monk dipped his quill in the inkwell and shifted gently to sit more comfortably in his chair. The only sounds in the scriptorium were the scratching of his quill on parchment and the purring of the white cat curled up on the monk's lap. The animal was Pangur Bán and the monk loved him. Loved him so much, in fact, that he neglected his work of writing holy words, and instead wrote a poem about his cat.

This was in the ninth century and we do not know the monk's name. His poem runs to eight verses in Old Irish and the lines compare the cat's happy hunting with the monk's own scholarly pursuits. The cat chases mice with the same concentration and avidity as the monk goes after truth in his writings. The poem, preserved in the Reichenau Primer, clearly shows the bond shared by author and cat, the comfort they bring each other and mutual companionship. While the monkish author's name has been lost in the mists of time, his poem has survived, along with his love for his feline friend. Through the centuries, the medieval poetic manuscript has inspired translations, musical renditions, novels, a picture book, modern poetic versions and even an animated movie.

Since cats were first domesticated and since human beings first began to write, there has been a happy conjunction between authors and felines. Writing is a solitary task and the companionship of a cat can be a relief, a comfort and an inspiration to authors. Cats are silent creatures; they don't need to be taken for walks, which might interrupt a sudden flow of creativity; stroking a cat's soft fur provides pleasure without distraction; and a cat can also provide a gentle nudge back to reality when a writer is lost in their imagined world. Studies show that cat ownership reduces stress, and writing can be a stressful task. Like cats, writers are sharp observers, so fellow feeling develops between the writer who watches and the cat whose green eyes unblinkingly watch his or her world. The symbiotic relationship between writer and cat illustrates our desire for compatibility with those who share our living space. And when writer's block impedes progress, then perhaps inspiration can be found by turning one's thoughts to a beloved feline companion? Cats even function as alarm clocks, with their need for breakfast rousing a sleepy author from bed. No other animal combines so successfully intelligence, insouciance and inscrutability, all wrapped in a soft and elegant package. The elusiveness of cats, their changeability as they switch from loving pet to ferocious predator, is part of their appeal to craftsmen trying to grasp a fictional world, or capture exactly the right word. The fastidiousness of cats is understood by a person fastidious about words. It's hardly surprising that, throughout history, puss has been permitted to sit on manuscripts, curl up on desks, take swipes at moving pens and sit on an author's lap.

That Irish monk was not alone in his love of cats. When Edgar Allan Poe wrote, his tortoiseshell Catterina was curled around his shoulders. Jean Cocteau thought his cats visibly represented the soul of his home. James Herriot described the feline species as 'connoisseurs of comfort' in his vet stories,[1] while Raymond Chandler regarded his black cat Taki as his secretary. Ray Bradbury saw his twenty-two cats as an integral part of his creative process; Jorge Luis Borges wrote poems to his felines; Iris Murdoch observed her cats as a way of getting inside the heads of her characters. Haruki Murakami even promised to write a book *if* his publisher would cat-sit while he went travelling. Elinor Glyn's scandalous 1907 novel *Three Weeks* about sinning on a tiger skin was inspired by the animal magnetism of her cats, Candide and Zadig. Dame Edith Sitwell prized the fact that her cats never said anything foolish. Alice Walker shared her vulnerabilities with Tuscaloosa, who sat at her feet as she wrote. Stephen King felt forced to write a tale of terror after his cat Smucky was run over. So many famous authors have loved their cats, from Aldous Huxley to Anaïs Nin, Anton Chekhov to W. Somerset Maugham, Charles Baudelaire to Jack Kerouac, H.G. Wells to Gillian Flynn. Every good writer, it seems, needs a 'mews'.

Authors love wordplay and find delight in choosing puss's name. Choosing names for one's fictional children can be great fun, but human names generally need to be sensible and believable. The naming of a cat allows greater scope for whimsy. Albert Camus (a heavy smoker) called his feline companion Cigarette; depressed (and depressing) author Janet Frame called her cat Negative; Tennessee Williams irreverently called his puss Sabbath; while Mark Twain tried to shock his neighbours with Satan. Most writers have failed to follow T.S. Eliot's poetic advice in 'The Naming of Cats' that any self-respecting feline should have three names: one for everyday use, one that is dignified and particular ('Else how can he keep up his tail perpendicular?'), and lastly a secret name 'that the cat himself knows, and will never confess', so that you know, when a cat is deeply contemplative, that he is pondering his 'deep and inscrutable singular name'.[2]

Some writers use literary preferences when cat naming. Victorian novelist William Makepeace Thackeray named his huge grey tabby Nicholas Nickleby after his rival novelist's character, while another of his cats was Barnaby Rudge. French poet Théophile Gautier shared his home with Gavroche and Éponine, named for characters in Victor Hugo's *Les Misérables*. Kiwi crime writer Ngaio Marsh called her cat Ptolemy after the Ancient Greek author. Ursula Le Guin's cat was Mother Courage (title of a Brecht play), while William Burroughs named his cat Calico Jane in honour of fellow writer Jane Bowles. George Bernard Shaw hated his own name of George, but loved his own plays, and so named his cat Pygmalion.

Family also provides inspiration. American novelist and anti-slavery campaigner Harriet Beecher Stowe decided to name her Maltese cat Calvin, also the name of her husband. Théophile Gautier christened one of his many cats Madame Théophile because she lived with him on terms of conjugal intimacy, while Sylvia Plath, rather disturbingly, named her cat Daddy as a result of her troubled relationship with her father (eponymous subject of her famous poem 'Daddy').

Others have turned to history when selecting names. Thomas Huxley's tabby was Oliver, for Oliver Cromwell; Florence Nightingale (who published nursing manuals) had Disraeli, Gladstone and Bismarck among her more than sixty cats; British prime minister Edward Heath (also a published author) had Wilberforce; Virginia Woolf gave house room to Sappho; gardening writer Gertrude Jekyll had Octavius; Alexander McCall Smith is a willing slave to Augustus Basil; while V.S. Naipaul had Augustus. Judy Blume, writing frankly about teenage sexuality, had Chanel for feline company; Hunter S. Thompson called his Siamese cat Caesar; while Charles Bukowski piled on the names for his pet, the grandly titled Butch Van Gogh Artaud Bukowski.

It's not surprising that a writer who loves cats will include cats in his or her work. Poems, stories, plays, fables, novels and essays give us a wonderful array of felines. Poets have mourned the deaths of adored pets; novelists from Daniel Defoe to James Joyce have placed cats in their characters' homes (or islands); and short-story writers have made cats the main topic of tales. There are even books written from the cat's point of view, detective stories solved by cats, cats that talk (Beatrix Potter's Tabitha Twitchit is a charming example), cats that do amazing things in science fiction, and cats that go off into space.

Cats also provide a standard by which characters can be judged. As children we learn that Little Johnny Flynn, who put poor pussy in the well, is *not* a nice boy, while Little Tommy Stout, who pulled pussy out, is to be admired. Those who are cruel to defenceless animals are to be abhorred. Jo March realizes Laurie Laurence must be nice if he brings back their stray cat; governess Agnes Grey tries to teach pupils kindness to all animals; and a servant in Virginia Woolf's *Between the Acts* cannot turn away a starving cat, showing her essential goodness. *David Copperfield*'s Mr Dick refuses to 'swing a cat'[3] because it would hurt the creature. Cats have been used as indicators of character, metaphors, guides to a better understanding of a literary work, symbols of something deeper, and have even been dedicatees of literary works.

For writer and scientist Erasmus Darwin, admiring a cat developed one's aesthetic sense. Aldous Huxley advised any would-be writer to 'keep a pair of cats'.[4] A contented cat is really the perfect companion for anyone literary. This book discusses a variety of writers – English, Scottish, French, American, Canadian and Kiwi – who have found their lives and works enriched by felines. Each writer has had a favourite puss, one with a special place in his or her heart and, sometimes, writings. They have shared relationships not of domination, such as that between dog and master, but of the unspoken respect which comes from an earned affection. They have played with their cats ('Who knows if I am not a pastime to her more than she is to me?',[5] queried essayist Montaigne), fed and cared for them (George Sand ate breakfast from the same plate as her cat Minou), stroked and were warmed by them (Emily Brontë penned some of *Wuthering Heights* with ginger and white Tiger curled on her feet), marvelled at them (critic and historian Hippolyte Taine was certain that the wisdom of cats was infinitely superior to that of philosophers), sketched them on manuscript pages, and found inspiration from their cats for wonderful books and poems.

It has been said that dogs have masters, while cats have slaves. Cats have never forgotten that they were once worshipped in Ancient Egypt. They know their important place in the world and by the hearth. Those of us who love cats have happily become slaves to our domestic cat gods. This book will introduce you to a range of cats – ginger and tabby, pure-bred and moggy, savvy street cats and pampered pedigrees. It will also introduce you to the fascinating authors who were their willing slaves and show how each cat, through its individual charms, made its way not only into the heart of an author, but into the pages of literature. The paws behind the pen have been mighty indeed!

# HODGE
## for whom Dr Johnson bought oysters

*Hodge condescended to live with Dr Samuel Johnson, born in Lichfield in 1709, died in London in 1784, lexicographer, essayist, biographer, poet, playwright, editor and critic.*

The life of a cat on the streets of eighteenth-century London was a perilous business. In the Middle Ages cats had been demonized as the familiars of witches – they were considered sly, artful creatures, never to be trusted. It was believed that the Devil could transform into a black cat, and when a cat caught a mouse it was seen as simply a symbolic form of the Devil catching souls. Witches were thought to transform into cats; in 1484 Pope Innocent VIII is said to have asserted that cats were the Devil's favourite animal, and idolized by witches. Cats were often burned with their 'witch' owners, or drowned with them. Because the cat could not be trained to be as obedient as a dog, this was seen as further indication of its falseness and malice. For the most part, cats were suffered because they killed rodents, but they usually found shelter in barns or, at best, kitchens, and foraged for food as best they could. It was rare for them to be welcomed into a cosy parlour and petted.

Only a few intelligent medieval people recognized the worth of a cat. Some nuns recorded keeping them as pets; the occasional scholar recorded his love for a cat (like the Irish monk who wrote about Pangur Bán); but for most people cats were agents of Satan. The Church condoned cruel treatment of felines. European villagers often massacred their cat populations, and the torturing of cats was regarded as 'proper sport' for children. Cats survived because they killed vermin, yet received very little gratitude or loving care.

Animal cruelty was also the norm for the Elizabethans. Bear-baiting was enjoyed by King Henry VIII and his daughter Elizabeth I; cockfighting, ending with birds pecked to death, was popular street entertainment; and songbirds were penned in tiny cages. Wealthy Elizabethans had a fondness for exotic pets – monkeys, eagles, apes and peacocks – but the cat had extremely low status in their eyes.

There was still no understanding of the way in which rats carried the fleas which passed on bubonic plague, but during the Great Plague of the 1660s the destruction of all dogs and cats in London was ordered. Daniel Defoe put the number of dogs killed at 40,000, and the number of cats at five times that figure. No accurate counting was done, but it's safe to assume that a huge number of London's felines met a brutal end in that decade. Cats soon crept back and were tolerated because, even if there was no understanding of how the plague was passed on, people still knew that if a cat was nearby fewer rats would raid the larder, 'bite the babies in their cradles',[1] and raid grain stores and provisions. Restoration diarist Samuel Pepys, who had pet dogs, canaries, a monkey and a blackbird, complained bitterly about being woken by yowling alley cats.

Things had not greatly improved for cats by the 1700s. Cats were sometimes skinned alive so their fur could be used for rugs (it was believed that if the poor beast was alive during skinning, the quality of the fur would be improved). In the ghastly sport of bull-baiting, cats were sometimes tied to the bull's tail so the beast would be further maddened by frantic feline struggles. Cats were rarely fed, or officially 'owned', in Georgian times, but were simply left to scavenge, breed and die in the streets, uncared for and unloved. No laws protected them. The Animal Protection Act came into being in 1835, but only outlawed bear-baiting, cockfighting and other brutal sports (although many continued surreptitiously). Most people in Britain believed that the Almighty had made animals for the fun or sporting recreation of mankind.

Throughout the eighteenth century, an era known as 'the Enlightenment', attitudes to cats slowly improved.

It was argued that if Man was top of the hierarchy, then he should treat those beneath him with humanity. The Georgians adored dogs which could assist in hunting, ratting, retrieving and were loyal, biddable companions, but throughout the century cats slowly came to be regarded more tolerantly and sometimes even affectionately, and the keeping of indoor pets, among the wealthy, grew more common. *The Cries of London*, a series of pictures depicting itinerant street-sellers at the very start of the nineteenth century, includes a vendor selling food especially for dogs and cats. Domestic cats began to appear in art (although this happened far more often in France than it did in Britain) and feline companionship slowly came to be viewed positively, rather than as something demonic. By the Victorian era it was thought there was one cat to every ten Londoners (London's population was then about 2.3 million), but few of these animals were cherished pets. They just lived as best they could on streets where they had to face the dangers of moving horses and carts, gangs of boys who tortured cats, hungry dogs, and many other perils.

But one cat was fortunate and escaped these horrors. His name was Hodge (a word used in the eighteenth century as an affectionate and typical name for an agricultural labourer), and he moved in to a house in Gough Square, London. There he took as devoted slave one of the greatest men of the century, benefactor to literature, and one of the most quoted of all authors – Dr Samuel Johnson. Hodge became a beloved companion, was well-fed, pampered and invariably treated kindly. In the Gough Square residence, just off Fleet Street, Hodge witnessed the birth of the first proper dictionary of the English language. Probably he sat on its pages as they lay around the attic. I'd love to be able to report that Hodge made himself comfortable right on top of the *C* page that defined 'cat' as 'A domestick animal that catches mice, commonly reckoned by naturalists the lowest order of the leonine species',[2] but sadly there is no definite record of his doing so.

Samuel Johnson was born in Lichfield, a cathedral city in Staffordshire, in 1709. He was the son of a humble bookseller. Yet Johnson rose to become a great literary figure. Throughout his life he loved cats, and was unusual for his era in his wish for felines to be treated humanely and shown affection.

Johnson married in 1735. His wife, Elizabeth (always known as Tetty), formerly a widow, was more than twenty years older than her husband. She did not share his love of cats and he had to remonstrate with her when she once struck one in front of her maid. Not only was such an action unkind to the cat, but it set a bad example to the employee, who might copy her mistress's example. After rejecting the bookselling occupation of his father, and trying his hand at teaching, Johnson moved to London, arriving there in March 1737. He took rooms in Exeter

Street, off The Strand, with a staymaker, Mr Norris (who had Lichfield connections), and his wife Esther. Johnson noted the good looks of his landlady (it was a while before Tetty joined him in the capital) and, with just as much approval, noted her dear little cat. Cats tended to lavish attention on Johnson, so it's to be hoped that during his many moves around London he often found rental accommodation that included a cat. He struggled to earn a living as a writer and was often lonely.

In 1748 Johnson and Tetty moved to 17 Gough Square, conveniently close to the printer of the *Dictionary*, William Strahan. Johnson had been approached by a group of publishers with the idea of creating the first authoritative English dictionary. Initially he anticipated the project would take three years, but it took him eight and was a mammoth task. It ranks as one of the greatest feats of scholarship ever performed by one individual, and for more than 150 years was the most commonly used and imitated dictionary of English. With its absorbing quotations, its sometimes highly personal definitions and the breadth of knowledge and literature it displays, Johnson's *Dictionary of the English Language* is not simply a reference book but a superb work of literature.

Tetty died in 1752. It is to be hoped that Johnson had a cat to comfort him at this sad time. In 1763 he met his future biographer. James Boswell was Scottish, young, ambitious, eager for literary fame, and something of

a 'collector' of famous men. With the plan of a future
biography in mind, Boswell began noting down Johnson's
sayings, strange habits and activities. His *Life of Samuel
Johnson*, published in two volumes in 1791, is considered
a classic of the genre. It set new standards in modern
biography, for it was not hagiographic, instead giving the
reading public a 'warts and all' picture of the man. Boswell
had many faults, but it is thanks to him that we know about
Hodge, for he recorded Johnson's love of his pet in volume
2 of the biography:

> I am, unluckily, one of those who have an antipathy to a
> cat, so that I am uneasy when in the room with one; and I
> own, I frequently suffered a good deal from the presence
> of this same Hodge. I recollect him one day scrambling
> up Dr Johnson's breast, apparently with much satisfaction,
> while my friend smiling and half-whistling, rubbed down
> his back, and pulled him by the tail; and when I observed
> he was a fine cat, saying 'why yes, Sir, but I have had cats
> whom I liked better than this'; and then as if perceiving
> Hodge to be out of countenance, adding, 'but he is a very
> fine cat, a very fine cat indeed'.[3]

Boswell suspected cats of displaying contemptuous
knowledge. Perhaps he felt Johnson's pet was looking
down on him, something which he, as a vain man, would
not have enjoyed? Boswell also described in his biography
how Johnson, hearing of some young man who was
'running about town shooting cats', grew deeply protective

of Hodge and 'in a sort of kindly reverie' thought of his pet and muttered 'But Hodge shan't be shot: no, no, Hodge shall not be shot.'[4] Johnson was always eager to guard his dear Hodge from the perils of London life.

James Boswell was made uncomfortable by Hodge whenever he visited Johnson. He was probably not an ailurophobe (a person who panics even thinking about cats, and phobic when actually with one), otherwise he'd not have been able to cross Johnson's doorstep without extreme suffering caused by Hodge's presence. However, he clearly found it hard to tolerate felines. He once tried to explain his dislike to the philosopher Rousseau, insisting that he found cats treacherous, ungrateful and stubborn, because they were intelligent enough to understand orders and yet wilfully disobeyed them.

It is not known when Hodge first came to Johnson's home and whether he arrived as a kitten or fully grown. Johnson's neighbour Percival Stockdale wrote a poem about Hodge, and so we know the animal's colour: he was sable – that is, a very dark brown or black. A nineteenth-century engraving of Hodge depicts him as a tabby, but how accurate that is nobody knows. Johnson was deeply attached to his cat. Also sharing the house at Gough Square was a manservant, Francis Barber, rescued from slavery in Jamaica. He assisted with the *Dictionary* after Johnson had him educated, but he often caused Johnson considerable worry. It would have been normal for a man of Johnson's prestige, especially after his *Dictionary* was published, to ask his manservant to buy provisions for the cat. But Johnson wished to avoid wounding Francis's pride by sending him on an errand 'for the convenience of a quadruped'.[5] He also worried that if Francis had to regularly perform such a task, he might take a dislike to the animal whose needs sent him out into rain or snow.

And so, in spite of his shockingly poor eyesight, Johnson went out himself to buy oysters for Hodge at Houndsditch Market. Oysters were very cheap and plentiful in Georgian England, often hawked around the streets. Stockdale commented on the way 'the ruggedness of Dr Johnson softened to smiles, and caresses, by the inarticulate, yet pathetic expressions of his favourite Hodge'.[6] Oysters were clearly to Hodge's taste.

In 1759 Johnson left Gough Square, the house by this time being larger and costlier than he needed. He moved to Staple Inn, then to Gray's Inn and from there to Inner Temple Lane, living in small rented rooms. But space was always found for Hodge, no matter where Johnson settled. All the homes were within the same part of London, so when Hodge did venture outside he was at least in an area with which he was familiar.

But even the most succulent oysters could not keep Hodge alive for ever. As his death approached, Johnson again went shopping, this time for valerian, a herbal relaxant and aid to sleep. He was willing to try anything that might relieve the sufferings of faithful Hodge. We do not know when Hodge died, but in 1778 Johnson's friend Percival Stockdale published an elegy about Johnson's cat. This cannot, however, be taken as the year of Hodge's demise, for later, in his collected poems, Stockdale gave the date of the poem's composition as 1764. Johnson's good friend Mrs Thrale seems to have known Hodge, and she only met Johnson in 1765.

Stockdale's poem is a rebuke to each of us who fails to appreciate the niceness of a cat:

*An Elegy on the Death of Dr Johnson's Favourite Cat*
Let not the honest muse disdain
For Hodge to wake the plaintive strain.
Shall poets prostitute their lays
In offering venal Statesmen praise;
By them shall flowers Parnassian bloom
Around the tyrant's gaudy tomb;
And shall not Hodge's memory claim
Of innocence the candid fame;
Shall not his worth a poem fill,
Who never thought, nor uttered ill;
Who by his manner when caressed

Warmly his gratitude expressed;
And never failed his thanks to purr
Whene'er he stroked his sable furr?
The general conduct if we trace
Of our articulating race,
Hodge's example we shall find
A keen reproof of human kind. ...
Let virtue in thy bosom lodge;
Or wish thou hadst been born a Hodge.[7]

There would be other cats in Johnson's life. Lily, a 'white kitling ... very well behaved',[8] shared Johnson's home for some years. It is known that he was living with Lily in Bolt Court (he moved there in 1776) in November 1783. No doubt Lily was fed on oysters too.

Hodge's bones must have long ago turned to dust, but in many ways Hodge, this particularly famous literary cat, has *not* died. In 1997 a bronze statue of Hodge was unveiled by Sir Roger Cook, Lord Mayor of London. It stands in Gough Square, just outside the only one of Dr Johnson's residences to have survived (today a museum) and depicts Hodge sitting, with tail curled around him, on a copy of the *Dictionary*. Next to him are some empty oyster shells. The pedestal, which is inscribed with the quotation about Hodge being 'a very fine cat indeed',[9] raises Hodge to shoulder height for an adult, so fans can put a friendly arm around him and be easily photographed in his company. A tradition has arisen of putting coins in the oyster shells for luck. The statue was the work of Jon Bickley, who used his own cat as a model. When it was listed in a children's guide to London, Gough Square received a huge increase in visitor numbers. To mark special occasions, such as Johnson's birthday on 18 September, a ribbon is tied around Hodge's neck.

Hodge has inspired authors as well as artists. Leigh Hunt wrote *The Cat by the Fire*, an essay featuring the imagined reactions of Johnson's friends to being told to purchase oysters for a cat. Actor David Garrick would have been 'too grand' for such a task; playwright Oliver Goldsmith, an absent-minded man, would not have thought of it; artist Sir Joshua Reynolds would have shrunk from the job; the philosopher Edmund Burke 'would have reasoned himself into its propriety, but he would have reasoned himself out again'; while historian Gibbon would have 'started with all the horror of a gentleman-usher' and immediately rung the bell for 'the cook's-deputy's-under-assistant-errand boy'.[10] In this scenario, only Johnson would have the lack of pride and practical kindness necessary for the task of procuring Hodge's oysters.

American writer Susan Coolidge (author of *What Katy Did*) wrote *Hodge, the Cat*, an ode published in 1912. It imagines Johnson, hard at work on his *Dictionary*, being interrupted by Hodge. Johnson must leave his lexicography and head to the fishmonger's to buy six oysters.

Hodge appears as a character in Samuel Beckett's early dramatic fragment *Human Wishes*; Nabokov's 1962 novel *Pale Fire* has as its epigraph Boswell's quotation about Hodge; in M.C. Beaton's Agatha Raisin detective series, Agatha is adopted by a stray cat in London – she names him Hodge. When a second cat joins them, he is called Boswell. Agatha is hopeless at cooking and lives on microwaved meals, but she is always scrupulous about feeding her cats well. In 1991 engraver and artist Yvonne Skargon produced an illustrated book, *Lily and Hodge and Dr Johnson*. In 2020 British author Robin Saikia produced a dramatic monologue, *A Very Fine Cat Indeed*, which has Johnson on stage reminiscing about Hodge.

In 2020 Southwark Cathedral named its adopted cat Hodge. Church authorities were certain that Hodge would want to stay because his master Dr Johnson is depicted in one of the cathedral's stained-glass windows (which was installed in 1907). Perhaps this Hodge will be the first in a long line of Southwark Cathedral Hodges?

Hodge was one of eighteenth-century England's luckiest cats. He witnessed lexicographic creation, he feasted on oysters, was pampered and petted, and he has become immortal because he deigned to share the home and hearth of the great Dr Samuel Johnson.

PAWS FOR THOUGHT
# Petrarch's cat

Somehow, in the public consciousness, authors and cats belong together. Readers have a mental picture of a cat curled up on a desk as the writer scribbles away, or perhaps of a cat purring contentedly on a lap while that author waits for literary inspiration.

This public desire for writer and cat to be co-joined has found the strangest form in Italy. Petrarch (Francesco di Petracco), whose love sonnets adoring Laura are formative works of world literature, did *not* own a cat – or, at least, there is no evidence that he did. He mentions dogs in correspondence but makes no reference to any felines in his life.

However, if you visit Petrarch's home (a fascinating literary museum and probably the oldest writer's house museum extant in the world) in Arquà Petrarca (perhaps the first town in the world named after a writer) you will see his cat. Not a plaster model, nor a picture, but an actual cat – mummified and displayed in gruesome glory in a glass case on the wall. The quotation below the animal comes as if written by the cat itself, glorying in having been the great love of the poet's life – Laura came a mere second. Petrarch died in 1374; the cat was first displayed in the sixteenth century. The then owner of the house had seen a fifteenth-century image of Petrarch in his study in which 'his' cat is depicted chasing mice. Tourists began visiting the house soon after Petrarch's death, and the owners appreciated the money they could make from them. Adding the enticement of being able to view Petrarch's adored cat was just another way of attracting literary visitors. French traveller Nicolas Audebert, visiting in 1575, was informed that the cat loved to accompany the poet everywhere. Lord Byron, who adored exotic pets himself, was delighted to see Petrarch's cat. Even modern tourists are fascinated by the ghoulish animal; Tripadvisor has many comments showing that today's cat lovers still rejoice in knowing that a famous author loved his cat. The internet has even mistakenly credited to Petrarch the words 'Humanity can be roughly divided into two groups: cat lovers and those who are disadvantaged in life' (it's not known who originally penned this saying).

Maybe Petrarch did once enjoy feline companionship? But whether he did, or didn't, it's safe to say that he'd be astonished by the strange 'birth' and 'afterlife' of the mummified cat that is today so firmly connected with his name.

# SELIMA
## whose death was memorialized for Horace Walpole

*Selima condescended to live with Horace Walpole, born in London in 1717, died in London in 1797, inventor of the Gothic novel, man of letters, antiquarian, art historian and Whig politician.*

When man of letters, writer, raconteur, art historian and originator of the Gothic novel Horace Walpole had the chance to meet Dr Samuel Johnson, he declined the acquaintance. Walpole disliked Johnson – his aesthetics, his Oxford education (Walpole was a Cambridge man), his slovenly clothes, his humble background (Johnson was a bookseller's son, while Horace was the son of Britain's first prime minister, Sir Robert Walpole) and especially his Tory politics (Walpole was a Whig) were all anathema to him. He had therefore no desire to be forced into conversation with Dr Johnson. Had these two important writers of the eighteenth century ever been made to meet, they'd have struggled to find peaceable conversational ground – politics, literary tastes, style of dress and how to socialize would all have been topics to avoid. The only topic that could have been safely chosen was the subject of cats. Although even there, Johnson might have found cause for argument, as Walpole, at heart, preferred canines to felines. And Johnson might well have disapproved of Walpole's rather shoddy care of his pets – animals under his protection had a remarkably high mortality rate, even for eighteenth-century pets.

Horace Walpole grew up with pets. His childhood home Houghton Hall, a Palladian mansion in Norfolk, and its huge park, were filled with horses, dogs and cats. Young Horace found it easier to show affection to animals than to humans. He especially enjoyed the unconditional love given him by dogs. Portraits of ancestors and relatives which also featured beloved pets adorned the walls of Houghton, so Horace took it for granted that animals would be part of his pampered life.

When young, he set off on the grand tour, taking as travel companion his friend the poet Thomas Gray (who wrote *Elegy Written in a Country Churchyard*). They'd been students at Eton and Cambridge together and had become friends, although were very different – Gray was withdrawn and quiet, while Walpole loved to socialize. Naturally, Walpole took dogs with him on the journey. However, he lost two of them in tragic circumstances. As the travellers were passing over Mont Cenis in France, little Tory, Horace's spaniel, was let out of the carriage to do his business. Suddenly poor Tory was seized by a wolf and carried off, never to be seen again. Walpole was deeply shocked by the violent death of 'the prettiest, fattest, dearest creature'.[1] But more disasters were in store. In Reggio, which they reached in May 1740, his dog Bettina fell from a hotel balcony and died. By this time, Walpole had only one surviving dog, Patapan, who had been given to him in Florence. Patapan lived to become the subject of his mock-heroic fairy story *Patapan, or the Little White Dog*, based on a fable by La Fontaine, which was only published in the twentieth century. Patapan managed to die from natural causes and Horace Walpole wrote poems in his honour. However, another spaniel, his beloved Rosette, died in a fire. It's hardly surprising that Walpole needed his own pet cemetery.

It was Selima's death that became famous, making the cat far better known in death than she ever was in life. Selima was a tabby;[2] she began to grace Walpole's London home with her presence around 1746. She was almost certainly named for a work of literature, as were many of Walpole's pets. In Nicholas Rowe's 1701 play *Tamerlane*, the feisty, cunning heroine is Princess Selima. Walpole, in 1746, wrote an epilogue for this play, and was immensely proud of it. Reminding everyone, through the name of his cat, of what he had written was a form of self-promotion, and Horace loved self-promotion. The other cat then sharing his life was Zara, almost certainly named for *The Tragedy of Zara*, an adaptation of Voltaire's play *Zaïre*. Other cats with whom Walpole shared his home throughout his long life were Fatima, Harold, Ponto, Selia, Sophy, Fanny and Mufti. But none of those felines ever gained the fame of Selima, who became the heroine of a famous cat poem.

Selima, Zara and Walpole lived at 5 Arlington Street, London, in a house given him by his father. Many government men lived in the area – so many that Horace referred to it as 'the ministerial street'.[3] In that residence, he happily collected antiquities, wrote letters (he was an assiduous letter writer), participated in politics and entertained his friends. As he ate, usually sparingly, he often shared food with his pets – dog, cats and even a pet squirrel were handed morsels of chicken or venison pie. Selima was the pampered pet of a wealthy and eccentric man and she should have lived a long and contented life. Thanks to a bowl of goldfish, that happy longevity was not to be.

The image of a cat gazing wistfully into a pond or bowl of goldfish is now very familiar. In *The Tale of Peter Rabbit* Beatrix Potter draws just such a scene; Dr Seuss's Cat in the Hat holds aloft a glass bowl containing one terrified goldfish; and Joy Cowley's *Greedy Cat and the Goldfish* also illustrates a cat seeking goldfish for dinner. Even comic-strip cat Garfield has been pictured looking hungrily into a fish bowl. But in Horace Walpole's day, goldfish were an exotic rarity. In the early seventeenth century they were introduced into Portugal, and from there spread around Europe where they were greatly prized. Dr Johnson's *Dictionary* fails to list or define 'goldfish', and the species was only first classified by Linnaeus in 1758. It is known today that goldfish should not be kept in bowls (this is often prohibited by animal welfare legislation as unhealthy because of the build-up of waste), but Walpole would not have known that, and thought the bowl made an ideal home for his pretty swimmers. Later in life he kept goldfish in a pond in his garden at Strawberry Hill (on one occasion, during a rainstorm, he panicked and rushed to bring his goldfish inside, quite forgetting that, as fish, they were used to water – the poor fish would have been more stressed by the handling involved in their removal than by the rain).

Horace Walpole was proud of his exotic fish, and he was also extremely proud of the bowl in which they swam. Like the fish, it came from China, dating from about 1730, so it was not old. It stood at 18½ inches (47 cm) high with a diameter of 21¾ inches (55.25 cm) and was decorated in a pattern known as 'The Three Friends of Winter', with plum blossoms, pine, bamboo and an arched bridge all part of its ornamentation. Chinoiserie was a current craze and chairs, teacups (tea was, by this time, very popular in Britain) and pictures in the Chinese style were highly sought after by fashionable society. Walpole had about 300 Chinese pieces in his personal collection.

Walpole kept this bowl, with its distinctive blue rim, inside his London home, placed near a large cabinet. It was fatally easy for Selima to climb from cabinet to bowl and balance on its rim, peering down into the water. One fateful day in February 1747 Selima scrambled onto the edge of the bowl to indulge in this favourite activity. From her precarious perch she watched the red and gold flickerings of the fish. Perhaps she lowered a paw into the waters in a futile attempt to catch one? Perhaps she was distracted by noise or movement? Whatever the cause of distraction, it proved disastrous. Selima slipped and fell, with a splash, into the bowl.

Her frantic mews went unheard by Walpole and his servants, Susan and Tom. Selima was unable to grasp the smooth, wet rim of the bowl. Gradually, exhausted by her attempts and chilled by the water (this was wintertime), poor Selima drowned. The golden fish swam around the corpse of this strange creature that had fallen into their aquatic home. We do not know if it was poor Walpole who found his drowned animal, or passing servants who first noted the gruesome sight. But, however the news reached him, Walpole was dreadfully upset by Selima's untimely death.

As a literary man, Walpole felt the need to memorialize his cat in words. An ode was, in his view, the most suitable way to express his grief and share it with literary friends. The macabre incident might well have been included in a Gothic novel, but Walpole had yet to introduce that literary genre to the world (he did so in 1764 with *The Castle of Otranto*), so a poem would, he thought, be best. The trouble was that Walpole was himself no poet. Fortunately, he knew someone who was – his old university friend and travel companion Thomas Gray. He therefore wrote (in a letter now lost) asking Thomas if he might consider penning a commemoration of the tragedy as a suitable epitaph to his beloved Selima.

When the two men travelled together in Europe, they quarrelled. The feud had since been mended, but Gray was anxious not to damage his fragile reconciliation with

'Horry'. So he replied from Cambridge, indicating that he was happy to undertake the task, but needed to 'know for certain, who it is I lament?' Was it, he asked Walpole, Selima or Zara who had drowned? Walpole had only stated that the tragic fate had befallen his 'handsome cat',[4] and Gray felt both were good-looking. Once informed that the unfortunate victim was Selima, he picked up his quill. What he wrote was far too long for an epitaph, but Horace Walpole didn't mind a bit.

Gray's poem had various titles in its first months, and some of the verses went through slight changes, but it is today known as *Ode on the Death of a Favourite Cat, Drowned in a Tub of Goldfishes*:

> 'Twas on a lofty vase's side,
> Where China's gayest art had dyed
>    The azure flowers, that blow;
> Demurest of the tabby kind,
> The pensive Selima reclined,
>    Gazed on the lake below.
> Her conscious tail her joy declared;
> The fair round face, the snowy beard,
>    The velvet of her paws,
> Her coat, that with the tortoise vies,
> Her ears of jet, and emerald eyes,
>    She saw; and purred applause.
> Still had she gazed; but 'midst the tide
> Two angel forms were seen to glide,
>    The genii of the stream:

Their scaly armour's Tyrian hue
Through richest purple to the view
   Betrayed a golden gleam.
The hapless nymph with wonder saw:
A whisker first and then a claw,
   With many an ardent wish,
She stretched in vain to reach the prize.
What female heart can gold despise?
   What cat's averse to fish?
Presumptuous maid! with looks intent
Again she stretched, again she bent,
   Nor knew the gulf between.
(Malignant Fate sat by, and smiled)
The slippery verge her feet beguiled,
   She tumbled headlong in.
Eight times emerging from the flood
She mewed to every watery god,
   Some speedy aid to send.
No dolphin came, no Nereid stirred:
Nor cruel *Tom*, nor *Susan* heard;
   A Favourite has no friend!
From hence, ye beauties, undeceived,
Know, one false step is ne'er retrieved,
   And be with caution bold.
Not all that tempts your wandering eyes
And heedless hearts, is lawful prize;
   Nor all that glisters gold.[5]

This poetic version of Selima's demise is an odd one – a strange mixture of graphic realism as the cat struggles in the water, along with classical allusions (nymphs, the 'genii of the stream', and so on), and a moral lesson against greed. It's a confusing poem, with its mingling of tragedy and comedy, and has been variously interpreted. Is it about the human mind trying to understand itself, does it concern perception, or is it, as some critics have suspected, a lewd poem, about a whore rather than a cat (with bawdy references now lost to modern readers)? The moment of the cat's death is chilling and all too real, narrated almost unfeelingly, which makes it read like a morality tale about the sin of lust for gold.

Whatever its exact meaning, the poem proved popular and was rapidly circulated among Walpole's friends. Dr Johnson, predictably, didn't like it, insisting that Gray's verses were like 'forced plants',[6] but others loved the poem when it was published anonymously in 1748. Boswell was an admirer – as a cataphobe, he probably relished reading about a feline drowning. Soon the *Ode* was being parodied, and parodies only work when the original is well known.

In 1753 the *Ode* was illustrated in a folio volume by Richard Bentley, with pictures taking precedence over the verses. *Designs by Mr. R. Bentley for Six Poems by Mr. T. Gray* proved important in progressing the art of book illustration. The pictures mirrored the mock-solemnity of the words. They are teasing, clever and elaborate, adding emphasis to the poem's themes. We see Destiny cutting the nine threads of the cat's life, cats wearing black headbands as they mourn Selima, and there's an illustration of a boat taking Selima across the River Styx (she looks displeased to see the dog Cerberus guarding the Underworld).

But Horace Walpole had not yet finished with his memorializing of Selima. Many pet owners would have got rid of the Chinese bowl which had proved a watery grave, but not Walpole. In 1773, two years after the death of Thomas Gray, Horace ordered a Gothic pedestal (somewhat like a church font) on which to place his Chinese bowl. This stood in the cloister at the Gothic extravaganza Strawberry Hill House, his Twickenham home, and can still be viewed there today. There's a label on the pedestal with the first verse of the *Ode* inscribed, so that no tourist visiting Walpole's home could forget Selima and her sad fate. Everybody visiting the recently renovated Strawberry Hill can learn of 'the pensive Selima' and her tragic death, nearly three hundred years after the event took place. That's not bad immortality for a cat!

Walpole returned to the subject of cats in 1751, when he wrote a fable, *The Funeral of the Lioness* about the King of Cats and the Lion Queen's state funeral. The work was in imitation of the animal fables of La Fontaine.

Walpole died in 1797, but Gray's poem lived on, continuing to inspire others. William Blake was commissioned to illustrate several of Gray's poems and created six hand-drawn designs for the *Ode*. Like the poem, these too are strange and muddled. Sometimes Blake depicts Selima as a woman, sometimes as a cat, sometimes as a mixture of the two – her face is often grotesque, with cat features beneath a lady's bonnet. Even the fish have human attributes. For Blake, Gray's poem was a story of the Fall – a vain young woman meets a terrible fate thanks to her vanity and self-absorption. Blake's designs were first published only in 1922, well over a century after he worked on them.

There's an oil painting, attributed to Moravian-Austrian artist Martin Ferdinand Quadal, depicting Selima perched on top of a glass bowl in which two goldfish swim. This work was created some time in the eighteenth century. Quadal ignored the Chinese vase (possibly he thought a glass bowl made it much easier to depict the goldfish?), an omission which would surely have displeased Walpole.

In 1944 artist and author Kathleen Hale created illustrations for Gray's poem, in what was planned as a deluxe Christmas edition. Kathleen Hale was a great cat-lover, who in 1938 had published *Orlando the Marmalade Cat*, which became a children's classic. That first Orlando book was followed by seventeen sequels. Her story of the marmalade feline came from close observation of her own cat: 'Orlando was very beautiful, striped like marmalade and the same colour; his eyes reminded you of twin green gooseberries.'[7] She brought that same close knowledge of felines to her work on Gray's *Ode*. She even used the X-ray of a cat's skeleton to help her get Selima's anatomical details right. Sadly, the planned edition was never published, so her seven illustrations remained hidden from public view.

Christopher Frayling's book *Horace Walpole's Cat* includes them, and they are charming, especially the one of dead Selima, resting on a bier clutching lilies, above the letters RIP. One of Hale's illustrations is used on the cover of Frayling's delightful book.

In 2015 sculptor Laura Ford created an outdoor sculpture installation for Strawberry Hill. The work, *Days of Judgement (Cats I–VII)*, featured large human-sized cats stalking the lawns, tails swishing, or slinking across the library floor. The art is wonderfully Gothic, suiting the style and atmosphere of the house. Selima, though, might not have been happy at such a feline invasion of Walpole's home – cats rarely welcome other cats who invade their territory.

The *Ode* written by Thomas Gray to memorialize Selima took on a life of its own and has endured. Anthologized, illustrated, set to music, painted and recited, it gave Selima a posthumous fame that few other cats have shared. Cats do tend to take human worship as their due, but surely even Selima would have 'purred applause' at Walpole's desire to memorialize her and at Gray's lasting poetic legacy in her name.

PAWS FOR THOUGHT
# The mad poet's cat

Between 1759 and 1763 a cat named Jeoffry shared the cell of an asylum with the visionary poet Christopher Smart, a friend of Dr Johnson. Abandoned by his wife Anna, who fled to Ireland with their children, tormented by religious mania, gawked at by sightseers who paid to look at inmates in St Luke's Hospital for Lunatics, Smart's only comfort was his feline friend. He kept himself busy during his confinement by writing *Jubilate Agno*, a religious poem of over 1,200 lines, most of it now forgotten by readers, devout or otherwise. However, 74 lines of the poem are among the most anthologized in English – those about his cat, Jeoffry, written as a sign of his gratitude. The lines today form a poem of their own, known as 'For I will consider my cat Jeoffry'. They delightfully describe the cat's daily routine in the cell:

> For having done duty and received blessing he begins to consider himself.
> For this he performs in ten degrees.
> For first he looks upon his forepaws to see if they are clean.
> For secondly he kicks up behind to clear away there.
> For thirdly he works it upon stretch with the forepaws extended.
> For fourthly he sharpens his paws by wood.
> For fifthly he washes himself.
> For sixthly he rolls upon wash.
> For seventhly he fleas himself, that he may not be interrupted upon the beat.
> For eighthly he rubs himself against a post.

> For ninthly he looks up for his instructions.
> For tenthly he goes in quest of food.[8]

Only a man who had closely observed his cat, day after day, could have written thus. The whole of *Jubilate Agno* is a Magnificat (a hymn, a song of praise to God), but the poem also forms a song of praise to one adored cat, a cat who gave poor Christopher Smart comfort when his life crumbled. Benjamin Britten set the lines to music.[9] Author Oliver Soden wrote *Jeoffry: The Poet's Cat*, a whimsical 'biography' imagining the cat's parentage and beginnings (in a whorehouse), and explaining how Jeoffry made his way to Smart's care. Published in 2020, it was much praised by cat-lovers Alexander McCall Smith and Hilary Mantel.

# RUMPELSTILZCHEN
## ruler of Robert Southey's 'Cat's Eden'

*Rumpelstilzchen condescended to live with
Robert Southey, born in Bristol in 1774, died
in London in 1843, poet and Poet Laureate.*

The writings of Poet Laureate Robert Southey are little read today as his works are out of fashion. However, ironically for such a lover of cats, the cat is not the animal for which he is remembered today. Rather, it is the bear – or, rather, three bears. For in 1837 Southey published the original version of a tale familiar to all children in the English-speaking world – *The Three Bears* – in which a little girl named Silver-hair enters a rural cottage and proceeds to taste the porridge, try out the chairs (she breaks one) and then falls asleep in one of the three beds. Later that child would come to be called Goldilocks, but it was Southey who first created the story and enriched literature for infants.

A later volume of his collected writings also included a memoir about the cats that Southey had known and loved at his home of Greta Hall. One of those cats was his favourite Rumpelstilzchen, or, to give him his full, grandiose title, 'Rumpelstilzchen, Marquis Macbum, Earl Tomlemagne, Baron Raticide, Waowlher and Skaratchi'. He was not a beautiful cat, being a 'mixture, tabby and white ... and the tabby is not good of its kind' but 'handsome enough for his sex, large, well-made, with good features and an intelligent countenance, and carrying a splendid tail, which in Cats and Dogs is undoubtedly the seat of honour'. Rumpel's eyes were soft, expressive and 'of a hue between chrysolite and emerald'.[1] Southey, already a dedicated philofelist (a lover of cats), was totally won over by this animal, who sat near him while he wrote, played with his children, and comforted him through some of the many griefs he had to endure.

Robert Southey, born in Bristol in 1774, educated in London and Oxford, rose to become Britain's Poet Laureate in 1813. He was friend to Samuel Taylor Coleridge, William Wordsworth and Walter Savage Landor, a prolific letter writer, historian, biographer (his 1813 *Life of Nelson* has rarely been out of print), a translator, travel writer, poet and, briefly, a Member of Parliament. In 1795 he married Edith Fricker, Coleridge's sister-in-law. The Southeys had eight children, but only four lived to adulthood. Southey supported his family solely through his pen. But he did not have only his own children to finance. Edith's younger sister Sara Coleridge and her three

children joined the Southeys when virtually abandoned by
Coleridge, and Mary Fricker, another of Edith's siblings,
also joined the household with her son Robert, when she
was widowed. Southey had to churn out books as fast as he
could in order to provide food and housing for them all. In
September 1803 they moved into Greta Hall, near Keswick,
in the Lake District. Southey initially didn't expect to stay
long; nevertheless, he remained there for the rest of his life.
When he died, at the age of sixty-eight, in 1843, he was
buried at nearby Crosthwaite Churchyard.

It was at Greta Hall that Southey was really able to
enjoy his 'pounce of cats', or his 'Cats' Eden'[2] as he called
it, and surely few cats have ever enjoyed a more literary
residence. From 1800 to 1803 it was home to Coleridge,
his wife and family – they moved in when the house
was newly built. In 1803 Southey came to stay with the
Coleridges. When Coleridge left in 1804, Southey stayed
on, paying the rent and coming to deeply love his Lakeland
home. Literary visitors included William and Dorothy
Wordsworth, William Hazlitt, Lord Byron, Charles and
Mary Lamb, Percy Bysshe Shelley, Sir Walter Scott,
Thomas de Quincey and John Ruskin. For any feline with
an ear for poetry, it was surely the perfect home. Robert
Southey was firmly of the belief that a house could never
be 'perfectly furnished for enjoyment unless there is in it a
child rising three years old and a kitten rising six weeks'.[3]
Greta was full of children, and before long full of cats.

There were cats at Greta when the Southeys arrived: 'I found the hearth in possession of two cats, whom my nephew Hartley Coleridge (then in the seventh year of his age) had named Lord Nelson and Bona Marietta',[4] Southey recalled in his *Memoirs of the Cats of Greta Hall*. Lord Nelson was a skilled ratter, so rapidly attained the honorary rank of Baron. As his skills at catching vermin grew even better, he was made a Viscount, and he eventually became Earl Nelson. He lived to a fine old age, but then grew enfeebled and unable to eat. As an act of compassion, Baron/Viscount/Earl/Lord Nelson was thrown into the river and drowned.

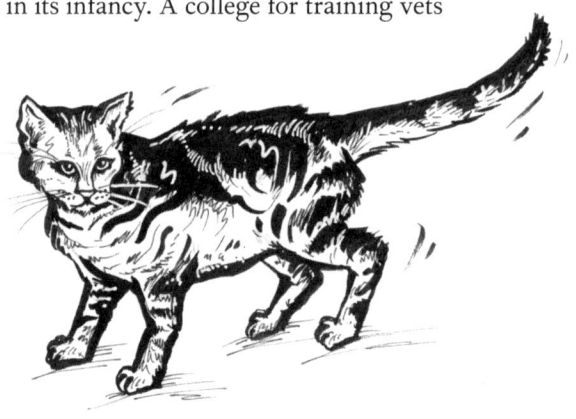

These days we'd take a beloved pet to the vet where the animal would be gently euthanized, going to sleep and never waking up. But Robert Southey had no such option for infirm Lord Nelson: veterinary science was only in its infancy. A college for training vets had been established in Lyon, France, in 1761, and in 1791 a London Veterinary College was started. But both establishments were centred on horses (the major form of transport and vital to agriculture), which were valuable beasts. The word 'veterinary' comes from the Latin *veterinae*, meaning 'working animals'. Cats were working animals in so far as they caught rodents, but they were seen as free-roaming and free-breeding; and if they fell sick they were simply left to crawl away and die. They were nowhere near as valuable as horses or livestock. While a London vet might conceivably have been persuaded to look professionally at a sick cat, it is more probable that he'd have regarded such a patient as a waste of his time or beneath his dignity. And Southey did not live in London – there were then no vets in country towns. Keswick was about one hundred years off having a local vet willing or able to treat domestic pets. Southey could have let Lord Nelson find his own place to die, but knew that might be a painful, lengthy process. He preferred the option of putting him into the River Greta – in mid-winter, that meant a speedy death. Drowning or shooting were the main ways of disposing of sick or unwanted cats in the early nineteenth century.

Lord Nelson, the original Greta cat, had many descendants, including William Rufus and Danayn le Roux. Southey's son Charles Cuthbert recorded his father's love of exotic names for felines:

> He rejoiced in bestowing upon them the strangest appellations; and it was not a little amusing to see a kitten answer to the name of some Italian singer or Indian chief, or hero of a German fairy tale, and often names and titles were heaped one upon another, till the possessor, unconscious of the honour conveyed, used to set up his eyes and look in wonderment.[5]

Bona Marietta, the other original feline inhabitant, was mother to Bona Fidelia, a tortoiseshell (at that time torties were sometimes called Spanish cats, in the mistaken belief they originated in Spain). According to Southey, Bona Fidelia 'approached as nearly as possible in disposition, to the ideal of a perfect cat' (but this was before Rumpelstilzchen entered his life). Fidelia died of extreme old age (outliving her daughter Madame Catalani), and was 'universally esteemed and regretted by all who had the pleasure of her acquaintance'.[6] Another of Fidelia's daughters was Madama Bianchi, always 'delicately clean', a beautiful green-eyed white cat 'with a fine tabby tail'.[7] Madama Bianchi unfortunately resisted domestication. She and her daughter Pulcheria were fed and indulged by the housekeeper, Mrs Wilson, but on that good lady's death both cats immediately skedaddled. Pulcheria died soon afterwards, while her mother was never seen by the family again.

For 'a considerable time ... an evil fortune attended all our attempts at re-establishing a Cattery',[8] Southey lamented in his memoir. Ovid disappeared, Virgil died from distemper (the classical names were chosen by Southey's daughter Edith), and poor Othello (who was, of course, a black cat) wandered into a busy Keswick street and there met an untimely end. Then Zombi simply vanished (interestingly, Robert Southey is credited with introducing the word 'zombie' into the English language, and also the word 'autobiography'). Prester John, soon after being named for the Christian patriarch, was found to be female, so had to be renamed Pope Joan, but suffered the very papal fate of death by poisoning. Poor Southey feared that the family might be 'at the end of our Cat-a-logue'.[9]

Southey wrote his memoir about the family's cats with the aim 'that the memory of such worthy animals may not perish, but be held in deserved honour by my children, and those who shall come after them'.[10] Unfortunately, he failed to add dates, so we cannot know exactly when the adored Rumpelstilzchen entered Greta Hall. He came as a kitten. At a nearby house lived a family called the Midgeleys, but they were moving away and so left an unnamed kitten with the Southeys, 'cats being the least moveable of all animals because of their strong local predilections'.[11] On the day of his arrival Southey had been reading his children the Grimms' fairy tale of Rumpelstilzchen, first published in German in 1812. The English version appeared in 1823, so perhaps that was the year of Rumpel's arrival in the household? Reading a fairy tale about the power of naming inspired Southey to give the new kitten his 'strange and magnisonant appellation'.[12] Little Rumpel settled in easily and was soon loved by all. An excellent rat-hunter, Rumpel too was ennobled for his vermin-catching services – he came to be 'His Serene Highness the Archduke Rumpelstilzchen'.

But another cat moved to Greta at the same time, one whose aggressive tendencies greatly disturbed poor Rumpel. This was Hurlyburlybuss (whose name was also of Germanic origin), a tabby who appeared one day and decided to stay. He 'made himself acquainted with all the philofelists of the family – attaching himself more particularly to Mrs Lovell'.[13] But Hurly was not fond of being indoors. Often, he'd disappear for days, leaving the Southeys wondering if he were dead, or even a witch in disguise. It turned out that other neighbours fed him and Hurly moved happily between homes, feasting in each. Hurly's eyes were 'between chrysolite and topaz'[14] in colour, and Southey described him as being of an ordinary size, and bad figure (probably the 'bad figure' was the result of the double rations he was enjoying).

The two felines lived in enmity. Hurly was master out of doors, while Rumpel reigned supreme inside. When Hurly attacked, Rumpel retreated into the 'citadel or sanctuary'[15] of the home. However, on one occasion Hurly fell sick. Rumpel, who had a lovely nature, made overtures of peace. Southey, ever fascinated by his felines, watched engrossed from the parlour window as Rumpel cautiously made amicable advances. Hurly received them with sullenness, much tail twitching and uneasiness. It was Hurlyburlybuss who, on this occasion, retreated, but once recovered from his indisposition he immediately resumed hostilities. Rumpel had, however, gained in confidence from that encounter and proved more willing to fight. Family members had to rush to interfere and separate the yowling, hissing cats.

While Southey believed that 'a kitten is in the animal world what a rosebud is in the garden',[16] it was indoors that Rumpel found the peace he craved. He spent his days 'in luxurious repose beside the fire, and looked for his meals as punctually as any two-legged member of the family'.[17] The housekeeper, Mrs Wilson, could not have purchased cat meat when shopping in Keswick; the first commercial cat food only became available in 1860, in London. Domestic cats were fed chopped meat, eggs, cheese, milk or cream (there was no awareness that dairy products were not good for felines) and, occasionally, cooked vegetables. Southey probably fed Rumpel bits from his own plate, possibly gave him chicken bones and offered him delicacies of ham or bacon.

No early-nineteenth-century shop would have sold such items as litter trays or cat litter. The Lake District is cold and wet for much of the year and Rumpel wouldn't have been keen to go outside to do his business (and face Hurly yet again). Probably the Southeys did what other Georgian pet owners did, and created a sand or dirt box. Neither sand nor soil are especially absorbent, so the indefatigable Mrs Wilson must have frequently changed the box's contents to keep Rumpel's lavatory facilities reasonably clean.

In spite of living the good life, Rumpel did occasionally fall sick. Southey described the challenges of persuading his pet to take medicine in a letter to his daughter Edith of 31 January 1825:

> His Serene Highness is afflicted with the mange ... [it was] prescribed for his Serene Highness that he was to be rubbed with a certain mixture, and take daily a certain quantity of brimstone ... The ladies of the Kitchen, however, are so interested in his welfare, that they have taken upon themselves the arduous task of administering the medicine; which is a matter of great difficulty and some danger, for his Serene Highness rebels against it strongly. Madam Betty takes him on her lap, and holds his head; Madam Mary holds his legs; and Madam Hannah stands ready with a bolus, which is inserted when he opens his mouth for a mournful mew.[18]

Three strong women were needed to make Rumpel take medication.

Even when travelling, Southey remembered his pets. In 1825 he was in the Netherlands, and wrote to his young son Charles Cuthbert (then aged six):

My love to your sisters and to everybody else. I hope
Rumpelstilzchen has recovered his health and that Miss
Cat is well, and I should like to know whether Miss
Fitzrumpel has been given away and if there is another
kitten. The Dutch cats do not speak exactly the same
language as the English ones. I will tell you how they talk
when I come home.[19]

Robert Southey does sound like an involved and truly
delightful father – what fun for his children to sit and listen
to Dutch cat language being spoken or growled! His letter
failed to mention the dog, Dapper, also part of the Greta
Hall menagerie.

Southey had a close friend from boyhood, Grosvenor
C. Bedford, who shared his love of cats – Bedford's pet
was named Dragon. It was with a heavy heart, on 18 May
1833, that Southey picked up his quill, dipped it in ink, and
passed on tragic news:

Alas, Grosvenor, this day poor old Rumpel was found
dead, after as long and happy a life as cat could wish for, if
cats form wishes on that subject …

There should be a court mourning in Catland, and if
the Dragon wear a black ribbon round his neck, or a band
of crape à la militaire round one of the fore paws, it will be
but a becoming mark of respect.

As we have no catacombs here, he is to be decently
interred in the orchard, and cat-mint planted on his grave
… I believe we are each and all, servants included, more
sorry for his loss, or rather more affected by it, than any
one of us would like to confess.[20]

No doubt Rumpel's bones are still there, beneath the soil.

Grosvenor Bedford was not the only friend who knew of Southey's love of cats. In 1824 he went travelling in the West Country and was there presented with an anonymous poem, purportedly written to him by Rumpel and Hurly. Probably the real author was John Marriott (1780–1825), curate of a Devon parish and also a poet. The poem was dated '*Keswick, January 9th*' and went on:

> Dear Master,
> Let our boldness not offend,
> If a few lines of duteous love we send;
> Nor wonder that we deal in rhyme, for long
> We've been familiar with the founts of song;
> Nine thorougher tabbies you would rarely find,
> Than those who laurels round your temples bind:
> For how, with less than nine lives to their share,
> Could they have lived so long on poet's fare?

The verses continue for many more lines, before signing off with: '(*Scratch'd*), Rumplestitchkin, Hurlyburlybuss'.[21]

His children and Coleridge's all understood Southey's love of cats. In 1851 a posthumous collection of Hartley Coleridge's poems was published by his brother Derwent. Hartley, as a boy, had lived at Greta Hall and had owned and named Lord Nelson. His cat-filled years at Greta Hall had only increased his love of felines. One of the poems in his collection, a work which would have pleased Southey greatly, was 'To a Cat':

> Nelly, methinks, 'twixt thee and me
> There is a kind of sympathy;
> And could we interchange our nature –
> If I were cat, thou human creature –
> I should, like thee, be no great mouser,
> And thou, like me, no great composer;
> For, like thy plaintive mews, my muse
> With villainous whine doth fate abuse ...
> And yet thou canst upon the rug lie,
> Stretched out like snail, or curled up snugly,
> As if thou wert not lean or ugly;
> And I, who in poetic flights
> Sometimes complain of sleepless nights,
> Regardless of the sun in heaven,
> Am apt to doze till past eleven –
> The world would just the same go round
> If I were hanged and thou were drowned;
> There is one difference, 'tis true –
> Thou dost not know it, and I do.[22]

Robert Southey had to face the deaths of some of his children (Margaret died as a baby, as did Emma, while Herbert and Isabel died at around the age of ten) and, in 1837, the death of his wife Edith. He did remarry, to the great consternation of his children, but seemingly more for convenience than from love. Caroline, his second wife, was also a poet, but it has not been recorded how she felt about cats. Within months, Southey's mental and physical health began to fail (he was almost certainly suffering from dementia) and he grew depressed. When he died in March

1843 Caroline left Greta immediately. Southey's children loved cats, so surely took in whichever felines were then resident and gave them homes.

Greta Hall is a Grade I listed building, currently run as a B&B. If you ever stay there, do think of Rumpel and remember the little kitten who was such an important and loved member of Southey's 'Cat's Eden'. Today cats with exotic names (Addleba, Vellyn and Noggin) still roam the property. If the shade of Rumpelstilzchen haunts the place where he lived such a literary life, it's nice to think his feline ghost has the company of other cats where he was once so happy.

## PAWS FOR THOUGHT
## The literary origins of the Tom cat

In 1760 a little book was published anonymously in London. *The Life and Adventures of a Cat* chronicled the doings of a London cat named Tom. It was the work of William Guthrie, but was narrated from the cat's point of view. The book proved immensely popular – indeed, so popular that male cats soon became known as 'Toms' or 'Tom cats'. The term has stuck and is still used today.

The word 'tomcatting', referring to promiscuous behaviour, also came into being as a result of Guthrie's publication. Dictionaries give a definition of 'tom cat' as 'a male domestic cat' or, in more informal usage, as a sexually aggressive man, or womanizer.

In the story, Tom is the kitten of Mab, who gave birth to a litter of ten. His mother, 'exhausted in spirits',[23] expired soon after. There is no record of his father, and all his siblings died soon after birth, but Tom tenaciously clung to life and became the property of Mrs Clotilda-Skin-Flint. She had poor Tom's ears removed and also planned to have him castrated, but as this was a troublesome and expensive operation she changed her mind. Tom earned his keep by killing rats and mice, and throughout the tale undergoes many misadventures in London's streets.

The Hanna–Barbera animated cartoons of *Tom and Jerry*, featuring Tom the cat and Jerry the mouse, resulted from Guthrie's book.

# MYSOUFF I
## who permitted Alexandre Dumas to escort him home

*Mysouff I condescended to live with Alexandre Dumas, born in Villers-Cotterêts, France, in 1802, died in Seine-Maritime in 1870, historical novelist, playwright, writer of travel books and a cookbook.*

In 1822 a young man left his home town of Villers-Cotterêts, 50 miles north-east of Paris, and set off to walk to the French capital. There was very little money in his purse, so he financed his journey by poaching, killing game as he went and selling it to innkeepers in return for a night's lodging or meal (he was an excellent shot). He had little in the way of luggage either, but his head was full of dreams, and he was ambitious to succeed in the world of the theatre. If he could write a play that would take Paris by storm, his dreams would come true. He left the Forest of Retz, where he'd honed those shooting skills and where several amorous adventures had been enjoyed; he headed south-west, and before long found himself in the bustling capital. He would indeed find success and fame, as a playwright and as a novelist, but Alexandre Dumas would also find a cat.

First, he had to find work. Thanks to the reputation of his father General Thomas-Alexandre Dumas and his illustrious career in the French army, young Dumas found employment in the Palais-Royal office of Louis-Philippe, duc d'Orléans (later Citizen King of France, 1830–48). Dumas had exquisite handwriting, so was useful to the duc when it came to the copying of important letters, but he had plenty of leisure in which to write articles and plays. He was only twenty-seven when his first play *Henri III and His Court* met with great acclaim. He found a mistress, dressmaker Marie-Laure-Catherine Labay, and she gave birth to their son in 1824 (Alexandre Dumas fils, legally recognized by his father, was a playwright, novelist and member of the Académie française). Dumas's mother left Villers-Cotterêts to join her son in Paris – they shared lodgings on the rue de l'Ouest, near the Luxembourg Gardens.

And that was the home where Mysouff I joined them in the mid-1820s. Dumas had a taste for the unusual, and many of his pets were given interesting names. In later life he owned a pet vulture, which rejoiced in the name of Diogenes Jugurtha; he had three pet monkeys and named one for a translator, one for a novelist and the other for an actress; but he left no record in his book *Histoire de mes bêtes* (translated as *My Pets*) as to why he selected the name of Mysouff for his white cat. Initially there was no number attached to his name – the creature later became Mysouff I, because he was succeeded by Mysouff II.

An unusual name was appropriate, as Mysouff I was a highly unusual cat and Dumas delighted in his cat's intelligent ways:

> The name of Mysouff had carried me back fifteen years of my life. My mother was still alive. I still enjoyed in those days the felicity of being scolded from time to time by a loving mother's voice ... I held a post in M. le Duc d'Orléans' service worth 1500 francs per annum. My duties occupied me from ten in the morning until five in the afternoon. We lived in the Rue de l'Ouest, and we had a cat called Mysouff. The animal had clearly missed its vocation; it ought to have been born a dog. Every morning I used to set out at half-past nine ... to return at half-past five. Every morning Mysouff escorted me as far as the Rue de Vaugirard, and every evening waited for me at the same point ... And the curious thing was, that on such days as some ... casual invitation tempted me to break my dutiful habits as a son and I was not going to come back to dine at home, Mysouff, though the door was opened for his exit as usual, positively refused to obey, and lay motionless on his cushion, in the posture of a serpent biting its own tail. It was quite different on days when I meant to return punctually. Then, if they forgot to open the door for him, Mysouff would scratch at it persistently with his claws till he got what he wanted. Naturally enough, my mother adored

the faithful beast; she used to call him her barometer. 'Mysouff marks my good and bad weather', she used to tell me: 'the days when you come, it is my "set fair"; those when you stay away, it is my "much rain".' ... Yes, I invariably found Mysouff on the look-out for me in the middle of the Rue de l'Ouest ... he used to dance about my legs just like a dog; then careering along in front, and turning back to rejoin me, he would start back for home. Twenty yards from the door, he would come back for a last look and then dash in full gallop. Two seconds later I would see my mother appear on the threshold.[1]

Years later Dumas acquired a black and white cat, and named him Mysouff II. At the time he kept an aviary of exotic birds, as well as some monkeys, and when a monkey left the cage door open the birds emerged. They found Mysouff II waiting for them and he killed every one, then began eating them. When Dumas discovered the tragedy, he put Mysouff II on trial, in front of the guests staying with him at the time. Mysouff II was sentenced to five years' imprisonment in the cage. But the sentence didn't last long, Dumas's financial circumstances being so dire that he was forced to sell the monkeys, and the cage. Mysouff II was freed without bail.

Cats appealed to Dumas because of their cleanliness, solitary and independent ways and their lithe agility and beauty. In his view, a cat was infinitely preferable to a dog because of its good manners, its feline grace and suppleness, and its ability to amuse anyone with artistic tendencies. He admired the streetwise talents of the cat, which could venture everywhere without getting lost, breaking nothing and, fastidiously, leaving no nasty deposits behind. To him a cat symbolized warmth and caresses. Even a cat's mouth was, to Dumas, a thing of beauty. Interestingly, for a man whose own love affairs were Parisian front-page news, he also loved the fact that cats hid their 'amours' from public view. He venerated a cat's pride and sense of self-worth — cats leave any home where treatment does not meet required standards, and they refuse to tolerate insulting behaviour. Dumas knew aristocrats from his career and social circles, but for him true nobility was found in 'aristocats'.

It's not surprising to hear that he named one of his cats 'Le Docteur' — feline softness and pride were, for Dumas, positively medicinal.

Mysouff I and II were almost certainly strays when they were fortunate enough to encounter Dumas. He often rescued stray cats from Parisian streets. Near the end of his life (Dumas died in 1870, at the age of sixty-eight) he formed a Feline Defence League. He'd have been aware of the Société Protectrice des Animaux (SPA), founded in December 1845, which makes it one of the oldest animal protection groups in the world.[2] Dumas encouraged authorial, cat-loving friends to be founding members. The brilliant short-story writer Guy de Maupassant, who wrote begging for better treatment for cats, and also wrote an 1886 essay 'On Cats' which describes 'the insecurity of their tenderness, the perfidious selfishness of their pleasure',[3] was a founding member, as was Anatole France, whose cat Hamilcar, guardian of his master's library from the predations of 'vile rodents',[4] appears as a character in France's novel *The Crime of Sylvestre Bonnard*. Poet Charles Baudelaire, whose poetic volume *Les Fleurs du mal* (*The Flowers of Evil*; when first published in 1857 the book created a public scandal) honours cats on several pages, was also an original member of the cat-protection society. Baudelaire suffered from depression and was known to completely ignore people if a cat was present. 'It is easy to guess why the rabble dislike cats', he once commented contemptuously. 'A cat is beautiful; it suggests ideas of luxury, cleanliness, voluptuous pleasures.'[5] How fascinating to have been a fly on the wall as those four extraordinary writers discussed cat welfare at meetings of their Feline Defence League.

Dumas's illegitimate son Alexandre Dumas fils (who gained fame with his 1848 novel *The Lady of the Camellias*, which inspired Verdi's *La Traviata*, and the movie *Camille*), inherited his father's partiality for cats. He too named a cat Mysouff, though whether he bothered to add the number III to the name has not been recorded. Loving cats, like writing novels and plays, was a Dumas family business.

PAWS FOR THOUGHT
## An author and the cat flap

There is a story that it was the great physicist Sir Isaac Newton (1642–1727) who invented the cat flap. According to what is probably an urban legend, the great man, up in his attic, was studying colour and the order in which it came in a prism, but his cat pushed open the door with its nose. The incoming light ruined Newton's experiment, so he decided to cut a small opening in the door and attach a piece of felt to the top of the opening. This meant the cat could come or go, with Newton continuing his experiments in peace. The idea proved so successful that he soon cut a second smaller hole for the cat's kittens. Biographers of Newton insist that he owned neither cat nor dog. However, an 1827 memoir by John M.F. Wright, a student at Trinity College Cambridge, Newton's own college, stated that there was in the door of Newton's old room 'two plugged holes of the proper dimensions for the respective egresses of cat and kitten'.[6] The story is probably not a true one – which is a shame. I like to think of Newton bending his great mind to the problem of his pets' comings and goings.

Notably, by an interesting quirk of history, Dr Nick Hill, a Cambridge physicist just like Newton, did invent the microchip cat flap. Unwanted cats were entering the house and disturbing his cat Flipper, so he developed technology which recognized Flipper's microchip but remained shut for any other cat. The first such product was sold in 2008. Dr Hill wrote a Ph.D. thesis in quantum physics, so can also be considered a cat-loving author.

*The Oxford English Dictionary* gives the date of the first use of 'cat flap' as being 1957, but the idea itself is an old one. In Ancient Egypt, where cats were revered, there are certain to have been holes made in walls which would allow a cat to enter, although without swinging doors attached to them. Geoffrey Chaucer writes of a cat hole in 'The Miller's Tale' in *The Canterbury Tales*:

> An hole he foond, full owe upon a bord,
> Ther as the cat was wont in for to crepe.[7]

# FOSS
## who owned Edward Lear

*Foss condescended to live with Edward Lear, born in London in 1812, died in San Remo, Italy, in 1888, artist, illustrator, musician, author, and poet best remembered for his nonsense verse.*

On no account could Foss be disturbed by a move to a new house. After all, he knew and loved every inch of the home that he and his slave Edward Lear shared at San Remo, an Italian town near the French border. And yet Lear felt he *had* to move. His glorious sea view was about to be blocked by the construction of a large hotel. There would be blasting of rocks, an assault on the ears and nerves of both man and cat, and the trees Foss loved to climb were to be removed. There was only one solution: the new house Lear planned to build further along the coast would simply have to be constructed in exactly the same design as the old one. That way Foss would still know his way around, would know which doors led into the garden, which rooms got the best morning sun, and his feline nerves would suffer no disturbance at all.

And so the new home was built using identical architectural plans. What had been the Villa Emily (named for a relative and also for Emily Tennyson, a woman Lear hugely admired) became the Villa Tennyson, and Foss and Edward Lear resumed the peaceful life they had lived in the other house, minus the problems of a new hotel. Together they strolled the garden, Foss continued to reign supreme on Lear's desk, and Lear enlivened the letters he wrote to friends with quirky sketches of Foss having fun. Edward Lear was a relatively late cataholic, but he was definitely an ardent one.

After a difficult childhood, Lear achieved success as an artist. For weeks he sketched and painted exotic birds at the zoo, and then published books on parrots and other species, which sold well. He produced an *Illustrated Alphabet* of animals and began writing limericks to amuse his friends' children. He travelled around Britain, sketching and then turning those drawings into pictures. At the age of twenty-five he set off for Italy to gather material for his *Illustrated Excursions in Italy*. This roaming lifestyle did not make owning a cat a sensible option, much as Lear loved animals (except for dogs, which he feared). In the next decades he travelled widely – Greece and Albania, Corfu, Turkey, Egypt, Palestine and Jerusalem. He had no wife to keep him in England and doctors advised that travel would be good for his health. Poor Lear suffered from epilepsy all his life. He apparently had some warning when an attack was imminent, and could shut himself away, for epilepsy was then little understood and was considered shameful.

But by 1870 he was growing weary of this itinerant lifestyle and felt the need for a permanent studio where he could complete pictures in comfort. He also loved gardens, and especially wanted a garden which would attract the birds he adored (birds feature often in his nonsense verse). In San Remo he bought land and found an architect; by 1871 Villa Emily was ready for habitation.

But what is a home without a cat? Lear's life had been a lonely one and he fought frequent battles with depression and loneliness. Though he never had an active homosexual relationship, his feelings for young men left him emotionally vulnerable and unhappy. A cat wouldn't be judgemental, nor embarrassed by an epileptic seizure, and would give Lear the love and devotion he could not find elsewhere. Or at least, that is what he hoped: 'I shall pay all my debts and if there is any overplus, buy a pleasing tabby cat.'[1]

The trouble was that Lear could not give up his wanderings all at once. After all, his excursions provided his bread and butter (not to mention cat meat). He needed to keep painting if he was to feed himself and cat. And it was his travels that meant his cat experiment failed initially. His first cat was Potiphar, an animal who came to Lear trailing interesting literary connections and was therefore deemed suitable for a writer's home. Lear's neighbour in San Remo was Lady Kay-Shuttleworth (separated wife of Sir James Kay-Shuttleworth), who had known Charlotte Brontë and Elizabeth Gaskell in England. She was a chronic talker and Lear had little time for her, but he did get to know the governess she employed for her children, Rosa Poplawska. Charlotte Brontë had found Rosa the most interesting person in the Kay-Shuttleworth household (how typical of Charlotte to seek out the governess). Lear loved *Jane Eyre* so would have been intrigued by Rosa's association with a novelist he so admired. It was Rosa Poplawska who gave Lear a cat. Perhaps, as a teacher, she knew that one way to make a lonely person happier was through feline connection? Lear promptly named his new kitten Potiphar, or Potta for short. Potiphar seemed to settle in well. 'The cat Potiphar is an eminent person in this establishment', Lear informed a friend. He soon experienced the ineffable pleasure of having Potta curl up on his knee. Soon the cat was following him around: 'Potiphar the unrivalled and excellent disports around the room', Lear recorded. Sometimes, kitten-like, he rushed outside to sit in an olive tree. For Lear, Potta was 'a model cat'.[2]

However, Lear and his servant Giorgio had a trip planned to Corfu (Giorgio's home, where his wife and children waited patiently to see him once a year) and Potiphar was taken along on the journey. Like most cats, he hated change. On Corfu he disappeared, never to be seen again.

Miss Poplawska, hearing of the loss when Lear returned to San Remo, came once more to the rescue, bringing over Potta's brother in 1872. This cat promptly climbed inside the chimney and had to be coaxed out, but he soon settled in. He was named Adelphos (Greek for 'brother'), but before long that name was shortened to Foss. As Foss, he became ruler of Lear's heart and household, and made for himself such a reputation that today Foss has his own Wikipedia page. How's that for cat celebrity?

It has to be said that neither Potta nor Foss was loved for their looks. Normally a cat's tail is a thing of beauty, curling and waving with immense grace as the animal walks. But Lear's two cats had only one tail between them, as a servant had cut off each cat's tail at half-mast. There was an Italian belief that if half a cat's tail was removed when the animal was a kitten, this would later prevent it straying. Lear had noted this cruel custom when in Rome decades before, observing that it was done so 'they will never forsake the house in which they have lost that useful member'.[3] With his tiger stripes and truncated tail, Foss was no beauty; as the years went by, his raids on the dinner table made him fat as well. But he soon gave Lear the companionship he wanted and the two became almost inseparable. Travels still had to be undertaken; when he couldn't face travelling without Foss, Lear tried to take his cat on a train, 'only Foss objected strongly',[4] so they stayed home. Lear had learned his lesson. If he travelled, Foss stayed at the villa, cared for by servants or friends, until Lear safely returned; or he simply didn't go away.

Foss soon ruled the roost. Before long he was in trouble for shredding letters (Lear had many distinguished literary friends – were the ripped epistles from Tennyson or Browning?). Foss was banished to the kitchen, but it wasn't long before he crept back to his accustomed place on the study rug, while Lear looked on dotingly, thinking Foss 'a good addition to one's lonely lonely life'.[5] Lear also blamed many messy ink blots on Foss, and the cat would roll on his manuscripts and crumple them – but he forgave him every time. Giorgio was not much of a cook and often put unsatisfactory meals on the table. Nevertheless, because Foss liked the man, Giorgio was allowed to stay. Lear shared his meals with Foss and often made such diary jottings as: 'dinner, Foss assisting'.[6] When visitors arrived, Foss slunk off to the back regions to check the guests out from a distance. When he emerged, it was to steal their toast, thus conferring on them his personal seal of approval. Sometimes Lear, when entertaining friends for dinner, created nonsense menus with silly cat dishes, as a way of honouring Foss. *Potage au Petit Puss* was followed by *Roti Gros Chat Noir*, *Pattes du Chat aux chataignes* and *Cotelettes de petit chat*.

Cats and birds are not a good mix, but Lear hated to be without birds, whose songs enchanted him. He reported on his pet's interest in his caged blackbird in an 1882 letter to his friend Lord Carlingford: 'Foss the cat, having taken to sit from 5 to 8 A.M. under the cage ... since that very charming animal took to singing, we had very great hope of our cat's aesthetic tendencies, and had expected eventually to hear poor dear Foss warble effusively. But alas! it has been discovered that there is a hole in the lower part of Merlo's cage, and Foss's attention relates to pieces of biscuit falling through.'[7] Even when Lear kept a canary, Foss never did learn to sing, but Lear credited him with many other marvels, often giving his beloved cat almost superhuman talents. He loved talking with his cat, even when the response was feline indifference or even rudeness. 'Walked sloppily on the terrace and discoursed with Foss', he recorded in 1877, 'who however was far from polite.'[8] He shared Foss's excitement when, one day, the cat nearly caught a wild duck in the yard.

Soon Foss was doing more than reducing Lear's loneliness – he was providing artistic inspiration as well. Pages of correspondence to friends and relatives (Lear wrote thousands of letters throughout his life) were more and more frequently adorned with charming caricatures of the cat, such as one in a letter to John Ruskin which Lear wrote in March 1886. When a young boy he knew in Italy, Charles Pirouet, fell sick, Lear spent hours creating an alphabet series to amuse the boy. The letter *C* for Cat was illustrated by a cartoon picture of Foss.[9] Foss caricatures also went into his 1888 book *Nonsense Songs and Stories*.

By 1871 Edward Lear had written his most famous poem, which of course features a cat of unknown gender. 'The Owl and the Pussycat' (in 2012 voted Britain's favourite poem) was written well before Foss came into his life, but the illustrations Lear produced to go with the verses depict a cat uncannily like Foss. Striped and with full complement of tail, the cat sits confidently in the boat while the owl plays his guitar.

In 1882 Lear produced a series of drawings, 'The Heraldic Blazon of Foss the Cat', depicting Foss in grand heraldic poses. These were a gift for his friend Strachey's little sister. *Foss couchant*, *Foss dansant*, *Foss passant*, *Foss rampant*, *Foss, a untin*, *Foss Pprpr* and *Foss regardant* are a charming testament to the enjoyment this lonely man took from watching his cat in different poses. However, after completing seven sketches, Lear felt 'it was a great shame to caricature Foss' and laid aside his pen. Sadly, no photo exists of Foss so we can't compare his actual appearance with the sketches. In the last photograph ever taken of Lear, in 1887, he posed with Foss on his lap. Foss, however, had other ideas. Just before the camera shutter clicked, Foss leapt up and fled, leaving Lear's arm still awkwardly positioned to hold him. The photo speaks eloquently of the cat that isn't there. As every person who has been owned by a cat knows, cats only pose when it suits them.

Lear was of course a writer as well as an artist, and Foss made his way into literary works as well. In an autobiographical poem, 'How Pleasant to Know Mr Lear', Lear wrote of himself:

> He has many friends, lay men and clerical
> Old Foss is the name of his cat;
> His body is perfectly spherical,
> He weareth a runcible hat.[10]

In 1884 he wrote a sequel to 'The Owl and the Pussycat'. The little-known sequel makes it clear that the cat is female ('Our mother was the Pussy-cat, our father was the Owl') – she dies and leaves children ('partly little beasts and partly little fowl'[11]), who must survive on their own when the owl is broken by sorrow over the cat's death. Cats also appear in Lear's limericks, such as the one about an eccentric gentleman:

> There was an old man on the Border
> Who lived in the utmost disorder;
> He danced with the cat, and made tea in his hat,
> Which vexed all the folks on the Border.[12]

But money still had to be earned by art as Lear never enjoyed real financial security. Sometimes he had to abandon Foss and paint the exotic scenes that sold well in England. Soon after Foss came into his life, Lear had the opportunity to visit India. An old friend had been appointed viceroy and Lear was promised vice-regal accommodation and exotic Indian travels. He set off in

1873, leaving Foss in the care of Hubert Congreve, son of his neighbour and a young man for whom Lear had great affection. He was away for well over a year – it's amazing that Foss didn't give up on him altogether. When Lear finally returned, Foss made his displeasure known. His first act was to zoom off to the cellar and escape the house through its broken window. He gradually adjusted, however, and man and cat resumed their old routine. Foss, though, was never happy when the suitcase appeared and the artistic materials gathered for a painting expedition elsewhere. Lear hated leaving: 'Poor old Foss came out to see me off, keeping close to me and butting me with his head',[13] he noted sadly; and 'Poor Foss would persist in following me right down the steps and into the road.'[14] He missed his cat when away, but the expeditions were a financial necessity.

Foss and Lear grew old together at the Villa Tennyson. As Lear became frailer, the cat was sometimes a danger to him. In 1880 he tripped over Foss in the dining room and hurt his nose badly. In 1885 he fell over the cat again. Giorgio died and was replaced by Luigi, and then Giuseppe, who cared for Foss and Lear devotedly. In a letter to Mrs Hassall, wife of his doctor, Lear joked that he had 'run a race with my cat from here to Ventimiglia, having beaten Foss by 8 feet and a half',[15] but their running days were over. Foss no longer raced up olive trees or tried to catch poultry; instead, he fell asleep 'in remote places'[16] and moved more slowly. Lear's sight was fading, he was disabled by rheumatism and he fell asleep often, sometimes with Foss on his lap, a favourite position for both. 'Foss always here',[17] he told a friend with satisfaction.

It was in July 1887 that the end came. Foss began staggering, stiff on one side of his body. Cared for lovingly, he lingered some weeks, but in early September Foss died. A grief-stricken Lear passed on the terrible news to close friends:

> For whoever has known me for thirty years has known that for all that time my Cat Foss has been part of my solitary life. Foss is dead: and I am glad to say did not suffer at all – having become quite paralyzed on all one side of him. So he was placed in a box yesterday, and buried deep below the Figtree at the end of the Orange walk and tomorrow there will be a stone placed giving the date of his death and his age (31 years) – (of which 30 were passed in my house) ... All those friends who have known my life will understand that I grieve over this loss.[18]

Lear, in his sorrow, got his dates seriously muddled. Foss was *not* a 31-year-old cat. Probably two when he came to Lear, he lived with him for fifteen years, and was probably either sixteen or seventeen when he died.

The funeral Lear gave his adored cat was more elaborate than his own funeral would be, only weeks later. Foss was given the elaborate headstone Lear designed, inscribed with the Italian words *Qui sotto sta seppolito il mio buon Gatto Foss. Era 30 anni in casa mia, e morì il 26 November 1887 – in età 31 anni* ('Here lies buried my good cat Foss. He was 30 years in my house, and died on 26 November 1887, at the age of 31 years'[19] – perpetuating the error regarding Foss's age). Lear, heartbroken at the loss of his pet, took to his bed. Two months later, on 30 January 1888, he died peacefully there. He was buried at the cemetery of San Foce nearby.

The Villa Tennyson did not survive. It was demolished soon after Lear's death. Foss's headstone now forms part of the foundations of a hotel swimming pool on the site. But Foss lives on – in Lear's wonderful sketches, in his limericks and in his letters. Those who loved Lear also came to love Foss. British singer Al Stewart mentions Foss in his 2005 song 'Mr Lear'. Foss is referred to online as 'a stumpy-tailed, portly, and unattractive tabby cat' who 'played an important role as a companion in the poet's lonely later years'.[20] What cat could ask for a better epitaph?

PAWS FOR THOUGHT
## The first book of cat care

Mary Anne, Lady Cust (1799–1882) was a naturalist, scientific illustrator and author. She grew up at Leasowe Castle in Cheshire, which interestingly was the home of the very first St Bernard dog brought to England.

Mary Anne had a passion for cats, with as many as a hundred living in a building adjoining the castle she inherited from her mother. She was a charitable woman – for example, when two of her Angola cats were sold at the Manchester and Liverpool Agricultural Show, she gave the proceeds to the local hospital. She owned a house in Madeira; when she travelled there each year, she took along her favourite Persian cat, in a basket locked with five padlocks. She'd had experience of a pet dog being stolen in the street, and didn't want anyone stealing her cat.

She was fond of doctoring her own animals and in 1856 she published the very first book on cat care – *The Cat, Its History and Diseases*. The book is thirty-one pages long. It begins by acknowledging the low status of the cat at that time. Some people felt it was presumptuous and undignified of Lady Cust to employ her pen on such a topic. Until this time cats had been left out of books on animal welfare and treatment – she wanted to rectify this omission. She gave recommendations on diet, how to administer medicines (anyone who has tried to make a cat swallow a pill will know that challenge), and she recommended cleanliness and warmth. Today's vets might look askance at her suggestion of laudanum for cats, but generally her book contained sensible advice. Some readers were impressed. As far away as Australia the *Sydney Morning Herald* enthused: 'At last the cat has been promoted to the literary honours which have so long been her due.'[21]

Mary Anne's granddaughter, Aleen Cust, is considered to be the first female trained veterinary surgeon in Britain, so an interest in caring for sick animals had clearly been passed down to another generation.

# BOB
## who helped Charles Dickens open letters

*Bob condescended to live with Charles Dickens, born in Portsmouth in 1812, died at Gad's Hill Place, Kent, in 1870, novelist.*

In the Henry W. and Albert A. Berg Collection of English and American Literature[1] in New York's Public Library (a library magnificently guarded by two big cats, the marble lions Patience and Fortitude) visitors can find a rather macabre item on display. It's a letter opener made from a piece of ivory for the blade, and a cat's preserved furry paw for the handle. Inscribed on the ivory are the words 'CD in memory of Bob 1862'. Bob, who was the cat once attached to that paw, belonged to the great Victorian novelist Charles Dickens; when he died his paw was used for this strange and slightly gruesome memento.

The Victorians were very keen on recycling. London's rag-and-bone men gathered up old clothes that could be sold to merchants or paper-makers, and bones that could be used in toys, ornaments and even for soap-making.

Victorians liked things to continue to be useful, and dead pets were no exception. There was a strong fashion for turning one's deceased pet into an object that could revive happy memories of the creature. Inkwells and snuff boxes made from the hoof of a loved horse, dresses and hats adorned with the feathers and beaks of canaries whose singing days were over, a tuft of animal fur set into a ring or bracelet, and even lamps made from the skins of dead pets – these were typical mementoes of the nineteenth century. Victoria's subjects loved curiosities, as did the queen herself, and filled their homes with unusual and sometimes exotic objects – an elephant's foot turned into an umbrella stand is one example.

The period of Charles Dickens's life (1812–1870) was also the golden age of taxidermy. In the Great Exhibition at Crystal Palace in 1851 a stuffed elephant fascinated the crowds. It was a full-time business filling Scottish hunting lodges with stuffed stags' heads, foxes and game birds. Dickens, when working on his last completed novel, *Our Mutual Friend*, visited a taxidermist's shop in London and was intrigued by what he saw there. He immediately created the character Mr Venus, a taxidermist who has stuffed toads, ducks, canaries and 'green-glass-eyed cats'[2] for sale in his dark and dingy shop. He even offers preserved human limbs among his assorted merchandise. In the midst of the dust and the death that surrounds him, Mr Venus of *Our Mutual Friend* is a wonderfully vivid character with a great connection to life. Dickens had his pet raven Grip stuffed and kept him in a glass case. But with Bob he clearly wanted a closer relationship. With Bob's paw turned into a useful object, Dickens was able to handle a part of his cat every day. He took the letter opener with him when he travelled and otherwise kept it always on his desk. Dickens received a vast amount of correspondence, so Bob's paw must have very frequently been in his hand.

Mourning was big business during the Victorian age, for humans and for animals. Cat and dog funerals were becoming formal affairs; undertakers were asked to create elaborately embellished caskets for animals; clergymen performed feline and canine burial services; and headstones were engraved with the details of family pets whose resting spots in the garden needed to be appropriately marked. When Bob died, Dickens almost certainly buried him (missing one paw, of course) in the garden at Gad's Hill – it was twenty years too early for the first British pet cemetery. (Hyde Park Pet Cemetery was created in 1881; Cherry, a Maltese terrier, was its first occupant. Over 1,000 burials took place there – mostly dogs, but cats, monkeys and birds were also interred, before it was finally closed to more burials.)

In spite of Bob and the letter opener, Dickens is more closely associated with dogs than with cats. He was a keen dog owner and during his life owned several different breeds. There was Timber Doodle, a Havana spaniel, and Mrs Bouncer, a Pomeranian. Generally, however, Dickens preferred big dogs (perhaps better suited to his larger-than-life personality); his favourite was Turk, a mastiff. A large dog collar once owned by Dickens (and marked with his initials) was sold at auction in 2021 – it was almost certainly Turk's. Then came Sultan, an Irish bloodhound, but Sultan upset everyone on his arrival by killing and trying to eat a blue-eyed kitten. He terrorized the neighbourhood and had to be chained up. When Sultan nearly killed a young woman, he had to be shot. Dickens at one time also owned a St Bernard named Linda and a Newfoundland called Don, then Don's son Bumble.

Dogs are plentiful in Dickens's fiction, Bill Sykes's Bull's-eye being one famous example, but cats are less common. There are over 500 references to dogs, but only a little over 100 to cats. Dickens doesn't give cats a good press. Krook in *Bleak House* owns Lady Jane, a menacing creature who sits on his shoulder and shadows him (although originally bought so Krook could skin her and sell the skin). Lady Jane watches poor Miss Flite's birds with avidity while 'winding her lithe tail and licking her lips',[3] leaving Miss Flite convinced the cat is really a wolf. Lady Jane slinks and lurks, and both she and Krook are malevolent and unpleasant. Owner and cat are well matched and Krook takes pride in his cat's viciousness. Lady Jane must have a lurking affection for him too, for, when Krook dies from spontaneous combustion, she sits mournfully by the ashes, all that is left of him. In an essay in *The Uncommercial Traveller* the cats Dickens describes roaming the streets around St George's Fields are 'sluttish housewives', wearing 'very indifferent fur'.[4] The essay uses the cat as a metaphor for a cruel and neglectful society. In his novels, cats are usually owned by women – Aunt Betsey Trotwood has one, as does Mrs Pipchin of *Dombey and Son*, but the animals are hardly individualized.

It was not only large fierce dogs that made Dickens's home threatening for cats. He famously owned Grip the raven as well, a bird that found a place in his 1841 novel *Barnaby Rudge*. When Grip died from eating paint, he was stuffed, and is now displayed in the Free Library of Philadelphia. Grip nipped people's ankles and totally cowed fierce Turk, but Dickens mourned for him and replaced him with Grip II and Grip III. He also acquired an eagle. An eagle or a large raven could easily kill a kitten, so it's not surprising Dickens was reluctant to have a pet cat in the house.

However, his eldest daughter Mamie (actually Mary, but always called Mamie) knew how to get around her father. On a visit to London she was given a white kitten and brought the little creature home. Dickens reluctantly allowed the cat inside and it must have learned to cope with the avian terrors of the house. The animal was named William, after Shakespeare, but when 'he' produced a litter of kittens a sudden name change was required. From that moment on she was Williamina. Her kittens were kept in the kitchen, but Williamina wasn't happy with that location for her litter. One by one she carried them into Dickens's study. On his orders, they were carted back to the kitchen, but she carried them all to the study once again, and again they were removed. After Williamina's third attempt, with the kittens placed at his feet, Dickens accepted the inevitable and permitted them to stay. Mamie wrote of their behaviour in *My Father as I Recall Him*, published in 1896:

> As the kittens grew older they became more and more frolicsome, swarming up the curtains, playing about on the writing table and scampering behind the bookshelves. But they were never complained of and lived happily in the study until the time came for finding them other homes. One of these kittens was kept, who, as he was quite deaf, was left unnamed, and became known by servants as 'the master's cat' because of his devotion to my father. He was always with him and used to follow him about the garden like a dog, and sit with him while he wrote.[5]

The cat did not remain unnamed. At some point he acquired the name 'Bob'.

Mamie provides no dates in her memoir about her father, so it's impossible to be sure of the date of Bob's birth. Dickens purchased the house at Gad's Hill (he'd admired the place when a boy) in March 1856 and used it as a country retreat until moving there permanently in June 1857, but possibly Bob did spend some of his life at Dickens's London home in Devonshire Terrace. Bob, sharing his study, must have met some of the great literary people of the day. Hans Christian Andersen came to stay, and Henry Wadsworth Longfellow, John Forster and Wilkie Collins were other distinguished literary guests. It's to be hoped that Bob appreciated such fine authorial company.

Being deaf, Bob could not hear himself miaow, so found other ways to attract attention. It is thanks to Mamie's memoir that we know about Bob's particular method of doing so:

> One evening we were all, except father, going to a ball, and when we started, left 'the master' and his cat in the drawing-room together. 'The master' was reading at a small table, on which a lighted candle was placed. Suddenly the candle went out. My father, who was much interested in his book, relighted the candle, stroked the cat, who was looking at him pathetically he noticed, and continued his reading. A few minutes

later, as the light became dim, he looked up just in time to see puss deliberately put out the candle with his paw, and then look appealingly toward him. This second and unmistakable hint was not disregarded, and puss was given the petting he craved. Father was full of this anecdote when all met at breakfast the next morning.[6]

Bob was deaf as a kitten, so must have been suffering from congenital deafness, caused by a genetic defect. The problem is pigment-related and is common among white cats. Williamina was white, but nothing is known of Bob's father. Judging by the paw, which must have faded in colour over time, Bob was off-white or grey. Some 22 per cent of white cats have hearing problems.

Artist and author Harrison Weir (author of *Our Cats and All About Them*, published in 1889 and considered the first pedigree-cat book) was charmed by Mamie's story and decided to draw a picture, depicting Dickens with Bob, who is reaching out a paw to snuff the candle.

Life can be a precarious business for a deaf cat. Outdoors it cannot hear approaching vehicles or other dangers. Mamie left no record of what brought Bob's life to an end, but Dickens was devastated when his cat died. If Bob was a kitten some time after Dickens moved to Gad's Hill in 1857 (he only used it as a summer residence until 1860), and then Bob died in 1862 (the date on the letter opener), he was still a young cat and should have lived many more years. It was Dickens's devoted sister-in-law

Georgina Hogarth who decided that a part of the cat should be preserved. It was she who ordered the letter opener made from the paw, presumably one of the front paws that Bob used to snuff his master's candle. (Goodness knows who was given the ghastly task of severing the paw.) The term 'cat's paw' means a person, or sometimes tool, used to carry out an unpleasant and dangerous task. Perhaps, rather appropriately, Bob's paw was used by Dickens to achieve his epistolary tasks until Dickens's life came to a close.

In 1862, the year of Bob's death, Dickens's publication *All the Year Round* published 'Cat Stories' by an anonymous author. The article insisted that cats, contrary to current popular belief, could display affection and respond to it, and should not be condemned as sly, selfish beings. Dickens, as editor, must have approved the piece being included and surely it made him think of all the affection Bob had shown him at Gad's Hill. The article used the phrase 'cat-fancier', meaning a person who breeds or cares for cats. This is the first recorded use of a term still in use today, after entering the world through Dickens's publication.

There is a saying popularly ascribed to Dickens – 'What greater gift than the love of a cat?' Today the epithet (sometimes with a question mark, sometimes without) is replicated on T-shirts, mugs, cushions and carrier bags. But did Dickens actually ever write these words? The saying does not come from any of his novels, letters or articles, and as a quotation can only be traced to the life of the internet. Is the saying simply a modern meme, created by someone who wanted Dickens to be seen to worship cats? If we admire an author, do we somehow need them to share our tastes and prejudices? Is it all a part of the faint sense of ownership we feel for a writer whose books have enchanted us? It's extremely doubtful that Dickens ever said such a thing, but it's now all over the web and plastered on merchandise – to those who do not probe any further, this saying indisputably belongs to Dickens.

So… was Dickens a 'cat fancier'? Only reluctantly did he agree to share his home with Mamie's Williamina and her progeny. But he was a sentimental man, deeply fond of animals, and a man who loved to observe all creatures. Somehow, a cat called Bob found a way into his heart and captivated the 'Inimitable Boz'.

PAWS FOR THOUGHT
## The literary Cheshire cat

In 1788 *A Classical Dictionary of the Vulgar Tongue* by Francis Grose gave the first recorded definition of a Cheshire cat: 'Cheshire cat: He grins like a Cheshire cat; said of anyone who shews his teeth and gums in laughing.'[7] Other writers, such as Peter Pindar and William Makepeace Thackeray, also used the phrase. People from Cheshire like to explain the saying as a reference to their abundant dairy farms, suggesting that the richness of the milk produced there would make any feline smile. Another explanation is that the crest of an important Cheshire family was a lion rampant, but when this was painted on local inn signs the lion looked more like a grinning pussycat. And there's a theory that cheese once sold in Cheshire was moulded into a shape that looked like a grinning cat. Today fanciful explanations abound, but it is generally felt that the phrase has never been satisfactorily accounted for.

In 1865 Lewis Carroll published *Alice's Adventures in Wonderland*, in which Alice encounters a Cheshire cat, who seems to provide a sense of calm during all her confusing experiences in Wonderland. She meets him first in the kitchen of the Duchess, and later she looks up at him in the branches of a tree. He is one of the few not intimidated by the Queen's constant threat of head-removal. The cat engages Alice in some baffling conversations and appears and disappears at will. This astonishing cat can make its head appear without its body, or can disappear gradually until nothing is left but its smile. Alice has 'often seen a cat without a grin' but never 'a grin without a cat'.[8]

There have been many theories put forward as to the inspiration for Carroll's grinning cat. Several churches he is likely to have known display carvings and gargoyles of grinning cats. Or it could have come from the term 'catenary' (the curve of a horizontally suspended chain, which suggests the shape of a smile).

The concept of a grinning, enigmatic, self-satisfied Cheshire cat has transcended literature and become part of popular culture in songs, video games, dating games, scientific phenomena, tattoos and cartoons. The famous cat even plays a role in linguistics – 'cheshirization' is when a sound disappears, yet leaves behind a trace. In 1951, when Disney filmed *Alice in Wonderland*, the Cheshire Cat became one of the first animated cats ever to appear on screen.

# BAMBINO
## whose slave was Mark Twain

*Bambino condescended to live with Mark Twain (Samuel Clemens), born in Florida, Missouri, 1835, died in Connecticut in 1910, novelist, humourist, lecturer, 'father of American literature'.*

Mark Twain was facing a cat-astrophe! Bambino, his beautiful black feline friend, had disappeared. His housekeeper had been spring-cleaning and, spotting an open window, Bambino had leapt out to chase a squirrel. And Bambino was not just any old cat; he was a walking therapist, a healing, soothing cat, and Twain needed him back – badly.

In 1904 Twain's adored wife Olivia Clemens (Livy) had died. The couple had been married thirty-four years and he was bereft. Their daughter Clara too was nervously affected by her mother's death and spent time away from her father on rest cures. Clara shared her father's passion for cats, so she decided she needed a feline companion to help her through her emotional breakdown:

> I had smuggled a black kitten into my bedroom, although it was against the rules of the sanatorium ... I called the cat Bambino and it was permitted to remain with me until the unfortunate day when it entered one of the patient's rooms who hated cats. Bambino came near giving the good lady a cataleptic fit, so I was invited to dispose of my pet after that. I made a present of it to Father, knowing he would love it, and he did.[1]

To cheer her, Twain wrote Clara letters about Bambino, telling her that the cat missed her and was even refusing his food, though probably, Twain concluded, he 'catches mice privately'.[2] In this way Bambino became Mark Twain's cat and his companion in grief after Livy's death.

When a famous writer faces a major problem, he or she usually turns to words. And that's exactly what Twain did when Bambino went missing. He advertised for his lost furry friend, offering a $5 reward to anyone who could return Bambino to his home. 'Have you seen a distinguished looking cat that looks as if it might be lost?', he asked hopefully in his advertisement. 'If you have, take it to Mark Twain, for it may be his.' He described Bambino as 'large and intensely black; thick, velvety fur; has a faint fringe of white hair across his chest; not easy to find in ordinary light'.[3] He asked responders to bring his cat to 21 Fifth Ave, New York. The advertisement was placed in the *New York American*. It had a fabulous response – hundreds of people turned up, clutching cats. The trouble was that none of them cared about bringing back Bambino – they just wanted a glimpse of the famous author. Twain's secretary, Katy Leary, recorded her surprise at the lengthy queue: 'My goodness! The people that came bringing cats to that house! A perfect stream! They all wanted to see Mr Clemens, of course.'[4] Not one of them carried Bambino, and Twain continued to fret over the loss of his pet. For a few days Bambino was a major news item and papers reported his disappearance.

Cats go about things in their own way, regardless of advertisements. Bambino, when he was ready (or hungry) did return home, three days after going missing. Katy heard a miaow across the street, and who should stroll in, unconcerned, but Bambino. Twain was delighted and immediately advertised that his cat had been found, but the stream of hopeful cat-holding fans continued arriving for many days.

Mark Twain and Bambino settled back into their companionable routine. With a cat on his lap once more, Twain could find some comfort in his life again. 'I simply can't resist a cat, particularly a purring one. They are the cleanest, cunningest, and most intelligent things I know.'[5] He loved Bambino for his independence: 'Of all God's creatures, there is only one that cannot be made slave of the leash. That one is the cat.'[6] He loved the feline's reserve and was certain that if animals had the gift of speech, then canines would be blundering and outspoken, while cats would know exactly when to stop and never utter one extraneous word. He delighted in his cat's naughtiness, certain that a cat was more intelligent than people suspected and could be taught any crime, and he paid reverence to its innate dignity, always letting Bambino go first when he opened a door – giving precedence to royalty, he insisted. Twain himself had enjoyed a rather wild youth, so perhaps it was the sense of wildness about Bambino which also appealed? In his view, cats were the tamest of wild creatures, yet also the wildest of the tame. He loved Bambino for his ignorance of moral dilemmas, his straightforward selfishness and his feline beauty.

Mark Twain had always adored cats. In *Pudd'nhead Wilson* he states: 'A home without a cat – and a well fed, well petted, and properly revered cat – may be a perfect home, perhaps, but how can it prove title?'[7] His mother, who taught her son kindness to animals (compassion to animals was rare in the Missouri of Twain's youth), often adopted stray cats. She'd have agreed with her son, who later commented: 'Some people scorn a cat and think it not an essential; but the Clemens tribe are not of those.'[8] The family also had dogs, but it was cats which won his heart. For Mark Twain, cats were an immediate passport to friendship: 'When a man loves cats, I am his friend and comrade, without further introduction.'[9]

His early years as a writer were years of travel – out west and then touring Europe. It was only when he settled in Hartford, Connecticut, with Livy and, as time went on, their three young daughters (a baby son died), that he felt able to provide a home to cats. And from then on there were many of them. At one time he was owned by nineteen cats. Felines became a significant part of his life. His daughter Susy later recorded the way her father loved cats in his own inimitable style:

> Papa is very fond of animals, particularly of cats, we had a dear little grey kitten once that he named Lazy (papa always wears grey to match his hair and eyes) and he would carry him around on his shoulder, it was a mighty pretty sight! The grey cat sound asleep against my papa's grey coat and hair. The names that he has given our different cats are really remarkably funny.[10]

Mark Twain's brilliant sense of humour certainly found an outlet in the naming of cats. He obviously enjoyed shocking his puritanical New England neighbours with the names he chose. One day, going to church, he adopted a stray black kitten, which he named Satan. Satan turned out not to be a tom, so had to be renamed Sin. Her two kittens were called Sackcloth and Ashes. There was Beelzebub, Famine, Pestilence, Soapy Sal, Stray Kit, Motley, Blatherskite, Babylon, Bones, Belchezar, Genesis, Deuteronomy, Sinbad, Zoroaster and Apollinaris (he once remarked that these difficult names were 'to practice the children in large and difficult styles of pronunciation'[11]). Twain liked to read German to his cats (he said it made them weep), and possibly that accounts for two names he chose – Germania and Fraulein.

One favourite was Sour Mash, who, he noted regretfully, 'cared little or nothing for theology and the arts'.[12] Of Sour Mash, 'that old tortoise-shell harlot',[13] he wrote in his *Autobiography*: 'Every waking moment was precious to her; in it she would find something useful to do – and if she ran out of material and couldn't find anything else to do she would have kittens ... She furnished us all kinds, all colors, with that impartiality which was so fine a part of her make.' Sour Mash killed snakes, mice, birds and grasshoppers, and if a dog came near the property she 'didn't wait for the formality of an introduction ... but promptly jumped on his back and rode him'.[14]

All his life Mark Twain was a keen billiards player. In fact, he considered a billiard table better than a doctor for bringing about a cure to any health problem. So, one of his cats was named Billiards in honour of the game. His cats were also fond of the billiard table – green baize made a nice place to sleep. Twain developed special rules for when his cats were on the table – a penalty was immediate if a ball chanced to hit a snoozing cat. He loved tucking a kitten into the pocket at one corner of the table, then watching its antics as it swiped passing balls. In a letter to a friend he described one such kitten:

> One of them likes to be crammed into a corner-pocket of
> the billiard table – which he fits as snugly as does a finger
> in a glove and then he watches the game (and obstructs it)
> by the hour, and spoils many a shot by putting out his paw
> and changing the direction of a passing ball.[15]

Even when on holiday, Mark Twain found it hard to manage without a cat. His solution to this problem? Rent a kitten, of course. In Dublin, New Hampshire, he rented three kittens for the summer. When he had to head home, he left money for the care of each of their nine lives at the end of the rental. His *Autobiography* records this custom:

> Many persons would like to have the society of cats
> during the summer vacation in the country, but they
> deny themselves this pleasure because they think
> they must either take the cats along when they return
> to the city, where they would be a trouble and an
> encumbrance, or leave them in the country, houseless
> and homeless. These people have no ingenuity, no
> invention, no wisdom; or it would occur to them to
> do as I do: *rent* cats by the month for the summer, and
> return them to their good homes at the end of it.[16]

On one occasion he went to a farmer's wife to rent a cat and was given a discount if he rented three, so he returned with two black kittens and one grey in his arms. For five months he took pleasure in them, noting when he handed them back that they were 'as full of romping energy and enthusiasm as they were in the beginning. This is remarkable. I am an expert in cats, but I have not seen a kitten keep its kittenhood nearly so long before.'[17]

Such a lover of cats could of course not resist putting cats into his books. He wrote *A Cat Tale* and *A Cat-Loving Family* (about mama cat Catasauqua and her beautiful family of catlings) for his daughters (these were only published in 1959) in which he had fun dreaming up more unusual feline names such as Cataleptic, Cataphonic, Catalonian and Catacornered. In *The Adventures of Tom Sawyer* there's a cat called Peter which Tom naughtily doses with pain-killing medicine. The result is electrifying:

> Peter sprang a couple of yards in the air, and then delivered a war-whoop and set off round and round the room, banging against furniture, upsetting flower-pots, and making general havoc. Next he rose on his hind feet and pranced around, in a frenzy of enjoyment, with his head over his shoulder and his voice proclaiming his unappeasable happiness. Then he went tearing around the house again spreading chaos and destruction in his path. Aunt Polly entered in time to see him throw a few double somersaults, deliver a final mighty hurrah, and sail through the open window, carrying the rest of the flower-pots with him.[18]

Aunt Polly suspiciously asks Tom what made her cat behave in such a way and Tom innocently states that 'cats always act so when they're having a good time'.[19] Aunt Polly forgives Tom after he tries to convince her how happy the medicine made poor Peter. Huck Finn seems to enjoy carrying a rigid cat corpse around with him for medicinal reasons, assuring his friend Tom that a dead cat is the perfect cure for warts.

In *The Refuge of the Derelicts* Twain writes admiringly of the independence of cats:

> That's the way with a cat, you know – any cat; they don't give a damn for discipline. And they can't help it, they're made so. But it ain't really insubordination, when you come to look at it right and fair – it's a word that don't apply to a cat. A cat ain't ever anybody's slave or serf or servant, and *can't* be – it ain't *in* him to be. And so, he don't have to obey anybody. He is the only creature in heaven or earth or anywhere that don't have to obey *somebody* or other, including the angels. It sets him above the whole ruck, it puts him in a class by himself. He is independent. You understand the size of it? He is the only independent person there is. In heaven or anywhere else. There's always somebody a king has to obey – a trollop, or a priest, or a ring, or a nation, or a deity or what not – but it ain't so with a cat. A cat ain't servant nor slave to anybody at all. He's got all the independence there is, in Heaven or anywhere else, there ain't any left over for anybody else. He's your friend, if you like, but that's the limit – equal terms, too, be you king or be you cobbler; you can't play any I'm-better-than-you on a cat – *no*, sir! Yes, he's your friend, if you like, but you got to treat him like a gentleman, there ain't any other terms. The minute you don't, he pulls freight.[20]

And in an unfinished novel, *The Mysterious Stranger*, Twain describes an encounter with a cat that could only have been written by someone with an intimate knowledge of their habits:

> The cat sat down. Still looking at us in that disconcerting way, she tilted her head first to one side and then the other, inquiringly and cogitatively, the way a cat does when she has struck the unexpected and can't quite make out what she had better do about it. Next she washed one side of her face, making such an awkward and unscientific job of it that almost anybody would have seen that she was either out of practice or didn't know how. She stopped with the one side, and looked bored, and as if she had only been doing it to put in the time, and wished she could think of something else to do to put in some more time. She sat a while, blinking drowsily, then she hit an idea, and looked as if she wondered she hadn't thought of it earlier. She got up and went visiting around among the furniture and belongings, sniffing at each and every article, and elaborately examining it.[21]

His story *Dick Baker's Cat* tells of a miner's cat called Tom Quartz who is adept at gold prospecting, but will have nothing to do with mining for quartz.

Mark Twain always kept an eye out for cats when travelling. In *Roughing It* he arrives in San Francisco and is greeted by throngs of them:

> I saw cats – Tom-cats, Mary Ann cats, long-tailed cats, bob-tailed cats, blind cats, one-eyed cats, wall-eyed cats, cross-eyed cats, gray cats, black cats, white cats, yellow cats, striped cats, spotted cats, tame cats, wild cats, singed cats, individual cats, groups of cats, platoons of cats, companies of cats, regiments of cats, armies of cats, multitudes of cats, millions of cats, and all of them sleek, fat, lazy and sound asleep.[22]

In a travel sketch about Westminster Abbey he recalls seeing a cat curled up at the feet of Queen Elizabeth I's statue, the sight of which makes him muse about human pride and mortality.

In his travel book *The Innocents Abroad* he notes the abundance of cats in Tangier; streets in Jerusalem so narrow that the local cats can jump across them easily; a cat in Marseilles' zoo which was permitted to climb up the elephant's hind legs and sleep on its back. And he notes with disgust the tale of a French ambassador to Tangier who made a carpet out of the cats he killed.

In 1877 he visited the island of Bermuda with his good friend Reverend Joe Twichell. Both men were fascinated by the names given to Bermudan felines – they encountered one called Hector G. Yelverton, along with Sir John Baldwin and, extraordinarily, To-Be-Or-Not-To-Be-That-Is-The-Question-Jackson. Twain wrote about these animals in *Rambling Notes of an Idle Excursion* and records hearing that Yelverton, 'a troublesome old rip', died in a trap set for rats, while its owner, Mrs Jones, demanded financial compensation. Sir John Baldwin met the same fate – he was owned by a Mrs Brown: 'She had a disgraceful old yellow cat that she thought as much of as if he was twins, and one night he tried that trap on his neck, and it fitted him so, and was so sort of satisfactory, that he laid down and curled up and stayed with it.'[23]

Twain's *Autobiography* is full of anecdotes about his cats, recording baskets of kittens in the hallway, the way he liked to eat with a cat tucked up close, his delight in stroking a cat, and his observations of their playfulness.

He did what he could through his writing to aid the new American Society for the Prevention of Cruelty to Animals (founded by his friend Henry Bergh) – *A Dog's Tale* and *A Horse's Tale* were fundraisers for that organization. He spoke out against vivisection and was a prominent spokesman for animal rights. He attacked hunting for sport, cockfighting and bullfighting. His very public views on such subjects did much to raise American awareness of cruelty to animals (he was much influenced by Darwin's *The Descent of Man*). 'Man is the animal that blushes. He is the only one that does it – he has occasion to.'[24]

Mark Twain had to endure tragedy throughout his life. Yet, in one sad time, it was Bambino who lifted him out of depression and helped him re-enter the public world. It's little wonder he reached the conclusion: 'If man could be crossed with the cat it would improve man, but it would deteriorate the cat.'[25]

PAWS FOR THOUGHT
## The literary hotel cat

In Midtown Manhattan is a hotel which has hosted so many literary notables that the establishment has become a New York City Designated Landmark. The Algonquin Hotel opened its doors to literati and theatrical people in 1902. It was the first major hotel in the city to accept unaccompanied females; it permitted guests to defer payment of their bills; and the owner, Frank Case, was known for helping struggling authors. In the 1920s it became the meeting place of the famed Algonquin Round Table, a group of writers, actors, wits and critics who met there regularly for lunch. Their wordplay and wisecracks were reported in the papers, becoming the stuff of legend and making the name of wit and author Dorothy Parker.

It was during the heyday of the Round Table group that a stray marmalade cat strolled into the hotel. The staff called him Rusty and kept him, but he soon had a change of name. Actor John Barrymore was a hotel guest at the time – he was there acting Hamlet, one of his most famous roles. He felt that Hamlet was a more dignified name than Rusty, and so Hamlet is what Rusty became. The Algonquin has kept that tradition and the current resident cat is Hamlet VIII, a ginger cat just like the original.

Hamlet is only allowed to be in the front desk area of the hotel (food serving regulations mean he cannot enter the restaurant), but he makes himself at home on luggage trolleys, behind the computer or in the lobby greeting guests. There's even a miniature chaise longue especially for Hamlet. He holds his own fundraising event every August – a cat fashion show. His portrait has been painted, he receives marriage proposals, has been given baseball caps, and there are people who book into the Algonquin simply because they want to meet Hamlet. Hamlet has his own email address and replies politely, wishing his correspondent 'a purr-fect day'.

But the hotel has never wished to be sexist in its choice of cats; there have been 'Algonqueens' in residence too. When a female is there, she's named Matilda. There have been three Matildas. Nobody has recorded why the name Matilda was chosen. It's a gorgeous tradition to have cats as resident receptionists/concierges of hotels – wouldn't it be nice if more hotels took up the custom?

# LA CHATTE
## who held Colette under her spell

*La Chatte condescended to live with Colette (Sidonie-Gabrielle Colette), born in Saint-Sauveur-en-Puisaye, France, in 1873, died in Paris, 1954, novelist, actress and journalist.*

In 1926 Colette, the famous French novelist, attended an international cat show in Paris. Such events were a relatively new phenomenon in France – the first had been held just twenty years before – and Colette, as a passionate admirer of cats, was eager to see what a cat show had to offer.

The very first cat show ever held had been in London two years before Colette's birth in 1873. This was a national cat competition at the Crystal Palace, and it attracted huge public interest (for the first time a Persian cat was seen by the British public). There is no detailed record, but it appears that somewhere between 150 and 211 cats were on display, and the public queued to admire them. Prizes were awarded for the biggest cat (he weighed

20 lb) and the fattest cat, and people saw for the first time many new, exotic breeds. Soon a second cat show was organized, this time permitting working men and women to enter their moggies for display. Two more shows were held in London, and Scotland also hosted a couple. The result of all this interest was the 1887 founding of the National Cat Club in England, a body which set standards for different breeds and chose judges to award prizes.

These shows initiated a feline frenzy in Britain, which rapidly spread to Europe. Soon cat shows and competitions were being held in capital cities – Vienna had one, as did Berlin. Paris, as a city that saw itself as a leader of fashion, couldn't possibly be left out. The first cat show in France was in 1896, and in 1913 the Cat Club de France was established. By 1924, however, there were ructions and the Cat Club de Paris became an independent body. That club established a stud book and register, the *Livres des Origines*. Famous people were frequently asked to be judges, to lend cachet to the events – novelists Émile Zola and Pierre Loti were two of them (both writers were cat-fanciers, so were well qualified to be judges). Most of the cat shows were held at the Jardin d'Acclimatation near the Bois de Boulogne.

In the late nineteenth century, public interest grew from simply admiring cats in shows to developing new breeds and collecting exotic cats. In 1869 only eight breeds were officially listed in *La Vie des animaux illustrée*. The latest trend among the bourgeoisie was owning distinguished cats, and Colette was no exception. What held her riveted at the show was a Chartreux cat (an officially listed breed), and before leaving she ordered a kitten from the breeder displaying there.

Chartreux are one of the oldest natural breeds in France. They are mentioned in a 1558 poem by Joachim du Bellay, 'Vers français sur la mort d'un petit chat' ('French verse on a kitten's death'). They are thought to have originated in a Carthusian monastery in the Chartreuse mountains in south-eastern France. They are a large, muscular cat with relatively short limbs, orange or copper-coloured eyes, and blueish fur (ranging from ash-grey to deep slate). Exceptional hunters, they were much prized by farmers. They are highly intelligent cats, which can be taught to do many tasks. Chartreux are known for their 'smile' – on account of the tapered muzzle. They are calm observers of the world around them. They look rather like the Russian Blue, a breed more familiar outside of France. After World War I steps were taken to preserve the breed, to which end a 'breed standard' was written. Generally, they weigh between 7 and 16 lb. It's the tips of the fur which give the coat a blueish/silvery sheen. The Chartreux is usually a silent cat, giving little chirps or small miaows when wanting attention. They are adaptable, observant and polite animals. Charles de Gaulle admired them and named his Gris-Gris.

Colette soon welcomed her kitten and named her La Chatte. This seems a rather unoriginal name to be chosen by a woman whose talent lay with words. Soon author and cat were devoted companions. Time spent with cats was never wasted time in Colette's opinion. She had loved cats since she was a girl; for her, no cat was ever ordinary. Her childhood home had always been a place for animals – in fact Colette's forceful mother Sidonie had 'boasted of her ability to housebreak pets and children'.[1] Once Colette was in her teens, her feline companion was Kiki-la-Doucette (Kiki-the-demure), a grey Maltese, and she liked to take him for walks on a leash around the village of Saint-Sauveur-en-Puisaye in Burgundy.[2]

In 1893 she married her first husband Henry Gauthier-Villars (always known as Willy) and they moved to Paris. But the move did not mean abandoning Kiki. Indeed it was her cat, her resolution to travel and see the French capital city, and her passion for solitude which were the invaluable things Colette took with her as 'personal belongings'. Kiki travelled with her to Paris, though struggled to adjust to an apartment lifestyle after the freedom of the countryside. The distressed animal 'roamed around depositing his wastes everywhere except in the designated receptacle'.[3] Her nickname for her new husband was also Kiki-la-Doucette, which must surely have caused confusion in the Willy household, but Willy took it as a sign of love, and felt honoured that she'd bestowed her cat's name upon him.

In 1900 Colette's novel *Claudine at School* was published under Willy's name,[4] and was an instant success. It was followed by three more popular books about the naughty schoolgirl. Claudine is given her creator's love of cats. Her cat is Fanchette, a cat of great character, though she looks ordinary. Fanchette and Claudine share a special bond and Claudine knows her pet wants sex as much as she does, 'so I asked round among the neighbours. The maid downstairs lent me a lovely husband for her, a fine striped grey.'[5] Soon Fanchette is expecting kittens.

When Kiki died in 1903, Colette was devastated. She turned to her pen as a way of dealing with her grief and wrote *Dialogues de Bêtes*, a quirky one-act play between Kiki-la-Doucette and Toby-Chien, Colette's French bulldog. This was published in 1904. Toby-Chien is loyal, rambunctious and devoted, while Kiki is standoffish and narcissistic, and the conversations between them are cleverly comic.

Colette separated from Willy in 1906 and they divorced in 1910. Husbands could come and go, but cats were a constant joy. Always sensuous and daringly modern in her choices of lovers, Colette rejoiced in the sensual nature of cats, the softness of fur, their rarely bestowed gestures of affection, their grace and agility. Cats were her muses and appear in many of her works. There's an old piece of Pathé film (which can be seen on YouTube) showing Colette, at the time of her second marriage, happily playing with her cats and a dog. Animals were vitally important in her life. She believed them incapable of deceit and far above humans when it came to integrity. She tried to emulate them and even once appeared on a dance-hall stage dressed as a wildcat.

In 1912 Colette married Henry de Jouvenel, editor of France's first daily newspaper *Le Matin*. He was somewhat astonished by his wife's passion for cats. 'One of these days you'll retire to a jungle', he warned her, adding 'when I enter a room where you're alone with your animals, I feel I'm being indiscreet.'[6] That marriage too ended in divorce – she had an affair with his sixteen-year-old son Bertrand, while Henry indulged in affairs with women who were less cat-obsessed and didn't make him feel an awkward third.

In 1925 she met Maurice Goudeket, who became her final husband. He shared Colette's love of felines and admired her almost religious fervour for animals. The letters she wrote to Maurice are full of the doings of her cats. It was Maurice who was in her life when the new Chartreuse, La Chatte, arrived as a kitten.

Colette was by this time an established and famous writer. *Chéri*, *La vagabonde* and *Le Blé en herbe* had all been published to great acclaim. In 1926, the year of La Chatte's arrival, she moved to an apartment in Paris's Palais-Royal, although she also had a country home in Provence. Her lifestyle was a nomadic one and she moved often. More Chartreux cats joined the family – Minionne, Pinichette,

Petiteu, La Touteu and Zwerg were some of them. Colette was often photographed at her desk, with cats in her arms. A photograph taken around 1938 shows her outdoors forming a relationship with a street tabby. Cats gave her aesthetic pleasure and comfort – her ideal of beauty was a sleeping cat. She delighted in her cat's beauty, the softness of its fur, its large unblinking eyes, the unrivalled loveliness of its paws and its twitching ears. Even delicate feline nostrils and curved claws that could scratch like thorns won her undying admiration.

In 1925 she assisted her friend, composer Maurice Ravel, by writing the libretto for his one-act opera *L'Enfant et les sortilèges* (*The Child and the Spells*). It includes a love-duet 'Duo miaulé' between Le Chat (baritone) and La Chatte (mezzo-soprano). Colette must have loved penning the dialogues, for the whole opera took her only eight days to write.

Her 1928 novel *La Naissance du Jour* (*Break of Day*) is strongly autobiographical. In it she celebrates the simple pleasures of life – one of them being an evening stroll along the coastal path with her coterie of cats. Her Provençal garden becomes a paradise because cats consent to spend time with her there.

In 1933 Colette immortalized La Chatte as Saha, the dainty Chartreux heroine of the novella *La Chatte*. She is much adored by a young man named Alain, who is as secretive and reserved as his cat. He bought Saha at a cat show because of her 'perfect face, her precocious dignity, and her modesty that hoped for nothing behind the bars of a cage'.[7] He loves her golden eyes, and the pearl-grey of her ladylike ruff. The two of them sleep together in his childhood bed. When Alain marries Camille, the new wife is jealous when she learns that she comes a distinct second to the cat. Camille is more like a large and energetic Labrador in personality — lusty in bed, demanding of her husband's attention. 'How could she be your rival?' Alain asks his wife. 'You can't compete with the pure; your rivals have to be among the impure.'[8] Goaded beyond endurance by Alain's words, Camille tries to kill her feline rival. She shoves Saha off the ninth-floor balcony. A fifth-floor awning breaks the fall and Saha survives. Camille must face Alain's fury — and she is the one who has to leave. She gets to keep the car, while he keeps the cat. When she looks back at him one last time, she sees him caressing Saha in the garden. Saha and Alain live together to their mutual satisfaction, with Saha 'purring full-throatedly'[9] to the end of her days. To Alain, his cat embodies childhood, which he is unable to leave behind him. Only Saha's death will end her hold on him. The novella's extraordinary version of the eternal triangle is rather disturbing. It was written in prose that Colette's biographer Judith Thurman describes as 'particularly feline — both detached and voluptuous'.[10] The cat is mistress and heroine of the story; while Colette shows little respect for Alain or Camille, Saha is obviously worthy of authorial admiration. As Colette wrote this work, she had only to look within the room for descriptions of Saha's appearance and behaviour. Saha is 'a little, innocent animal as blue as the best dreams',[11] faithful, fastidious – a replica of her own beloved La Chatte.

Weary of constant moves, Colette settled again at the Palais-Royal in 1938. It was in her first-floor apartment, with garden views, that La Chatte and Colette both spent their last days. By early 1939 La Chatte was ill with cancer and Colette sorrowfully had her put down in February. She vowed never to have another cat, even though she found it upsetting to be living without an animal for the first time in her life. Perfect friends are invariably four-footed was Colette's sad conclusion.

Colette, like a cat, had lived nine lives by the time she died in 1954. She was a Nobel Prize-nominated writer, a music-hall performer, an intellectual, a beautician (it was said women exited her salon looking ten years older than when they went in), a journalist, a lover of both men and women, a mother (although a very poor parent to her only child, Colette de Jouvenel, always known as Bel-Gazou), wife to three different men, and a lover of cats. People said that her eyes resembled a cat's, and she certainly had the independence and spirit of the 'cat that walked by itself'. *The London Review of Books* has described Colette as 'the frizzle-headed Cat Woman of 20th-century French writing'[12] – there are worse ways to be remembered.

PAWS FOR THOUGHT
# The cat of *The Incredible Journey*

In the 1950s the Burnford family, living in Ontario, Canada, acquired a Siamese kitten. At first they were worried that the new arrival would fight with Bodger, their faithful Bull Terrier, who had been Sheila Burnford's protective companion during the blackout nights of World War II. But they need not have worried, for the animals bonded amazingly well. The kitten was named Simon, and soon Simon and Bodger were inseparable. They even began assuming each other's characteristics while participating in forbidden behaviour, such as opening the kitchen door to get at food. Sheila had never seen such cooperation and closeness between a dog and a cat.

Bodger grew old and his sight began to fail, but the family acquired a new dog – a Labrador Retriever named Luath (named after poet Robert Burns's dog). Luath also got on extremely well with Simon the cat, and so loved Bodger that he accompanied the old dog on neighbourhood walks, sticking close by his side so Bodger could find his way home.

Her observations of the family's three pets gave Sheila Burnford the idea for a book, and in 1961 she published *The Incredible Journey* featuring Bodger the Bull Terrier, Tao the Siamese and Luath the Retriever. The animals of the story are left with friends while their owners make an extended trip to England (where Sheila had grown up), but they opt to undertake the 300-mile walk through the Canadian wilderness to find their own home again.

Although Simon, the Burnfords' cat, never made such an epic journey, Tao in the novel was based on Simon's looks and personality. Tao is a sealpoint Siamese with sapphire eyes. He despises other cats and when meeting any on his journey fights them successfully. Like Simon, he can open doors. While he can survive perfectly well on his own when separated from his canine friends, he is loyal and devoted and spends all his time seeking to rejoin them. He's a skilled hunter and is crucial to the survival of the trio.

When published, *The Incredible Journey* was only a moderate success. However, in 1963 it was loosely adapted in a Disney movie, which greatly increased the popularity of the book. In 1993 it was filmed again. Many readers thought the book was non-fiction, an idea which tickled Burnford, who joked that her readers must have thought the cat kept a diary. It was Sheila Burnford's close observation of her own pets and of the Canadian landscape which had made her story so convincing.

# DAFFY

## who knew Anne of Green Gables before anybody else

*Daffy condescended to live with Lucy Maud Montgomery, born in Prince Edward Island, Canada, in 1874, died in Toronto in 1942, novelist, poet and short-story writer.*

In 1892 Lucy Maud Montgomery jotted down a good story idea in her journal: 'Elderly couple apply to orphan asylum for a boy. By mistake a girl is sent them.'[1] This idea sat, unused, for some years, but in 1905 she returned to it, feeling that perhaps she could make more of it than one of the short stories that were currently her bread and butter. Maybe it could even be turned into her first novel? Picking up her pen, Montgomery began her story with the wonderful long opening sentence about Mrs Rachel Lynde, 'guardian' of Avonlea, and the brook which flows through the village, a brook which will symbolize the spirited heroine she was creating, Anne of Green Gables.

Montgomery's mother died when she was an infant. From babyhood she lived with grandparents, strict puritanical people of Scottish descent, who 'did their duty' by the imaginative little girl in their care but showed no understanding for her flights of fantasy, her passion for fiction, her interest in writing. Her father remarried and fathered another child; when he died in 1900 she became an orphan, like her character Anne Shirley. Montgomery was bereft of human sympathy as she wrote this first book.

However, she was not bereft of company. Daffy (officially named Daffy the Third) was with her throughout the 'birth' of *Anne of Green Gables*. Daffy sat on her lap as, huddled in coat and blankets in the early morning, she tried to keep warm as she wrote. It was Daffy who climbed onto her desk and sat on the precious manuscript (now held at Charlottetown's Confederation Centre), and it was this beloved large grey cat which gave her solace as she laboured over her story. Daffy was a constant presence as the tale of a red-haired girl, with a 'tongue hung in the middle' and a vivid imagination, progressed. Through Anne's arrival at Green Gables to her errors with cake flavouring and raspberry cordial, Daffy was at Montgomery's side. Did he sit on the pages describing Anne cracking a slate over the head of Gilbert Blythe for calling her 'Carrots'? Did Daffy spread ink by walking uncaring over Montgomery's moving description of Matthew's death? Did Daffy realize just what a fortunate animal he was to be present at the creation of such a novel?

Cats had been a constant in young Montgomery's life, always regarded as soulmates. She was a lonely child – cats provided much-needed companionship. Her journal, started when she was fourteen, chronicles her love of all the cats in her life. The Cavendish farm run by her grandparents had barn cats for the rodents, but those animals were never encouraged to enter the house. Somehow, though, Montgomery sneaked in her 'pussy folk':[2] grandparents 'never liked to see me petting cats but did not actually forbid my having one ... but they were a great pleasure to me and I loved them'.[3] As a child, she wrote elaborate 'biographies' of each puss. She never forgot the trauma of seeing her first grey kitten die (from poisoning) when she was a sensitive nine-year old – 'the agony'[4] stayed with her for life. The death of this kitten was her 'baptism of sorrow':

> If I had had a mother – a wise, tender mother – to take me in her arms and comfort me understandingly, not underrating the suffering through contempt of the cause, it would have been well for me. Instead, grandmother only said, sneeringly, 'You'll have something to cry for some day' and left me to sob my soul out in loneliness over the poor gray body of my little pet. I grieved stormily all that day and more quietly for weeks afterwards.[5]

There were many other childhood cats – another grey was bright-eyed Pussywillow, whom she loved 'with all the devotion of [her] passionate little heart';[6] 'meek and pink-nosed' Catkin;[7] as well as Mephistopheles and Lady Katherine. Her grandparents had Gyp, a dog who detested cats; indeed Gyp killed some of Montgomery's kittens. She tried keeping them in the granary where they would be safe, but Catkin simply disappeared. Gyp died when Montgomery was about twelve and it was then she got grey and white Topsy, 'a beautiful and intelligent cat'[8] who had kittens, one of whom was Max, 'just a beauty – grey, tiger-stripe fellow'.[9] 'He was a dear cat, but when he was about two years old he went away and never returned.'

After that, four grey felines held her affection: Coco, 'a pretty light gray, whose name I changed to "Bobs" in a fit of hero worship during the Boer War';[10] the second was dark-gray Daffy the First.'

> Then came Daffy the Second – a silver gray, the dearest and handsomest cat I ever had. All these died of poison. When Daffy the Second died I felt almost as badly as I had felt over Pussywillow's death long ago. Now I have Daffy the Third whom I got as a kitten from Alec MacNeill's. He is four years old, a very large, handsome fellow and stays home so closely that his days have been long in the land. I do not know what I would do without him. I would be ashamed to say just how much I love that cat.[11]

Another childhood cat was Maggie, who died when Montgomery was seventeen. She honoured that feline's death with a poem, 'In Memory of Maggie'. Cats brought

Montgomery peace and tranquillity, a sense of spiritual connectedness vital to her wellbeing.

Grey Daffy the Third came into Montgomery's life just before she started writing *Anne of Green Gables*. He was a Cavendish cat (Cavendish becomes the village of Avonlea in her fiction) so was an island animal, a part of her beloved Prince Edward Island. He was born in 1906, and Montgomery named him Daff-o-dill, then Daffy the Third, but that was rapidly shortened to Daffy, or sometimes Daff. He was tolerated reluctantly by her cataphobic relations: 'I have always been very fond of cats', Montgomery later recorded. 'I do not know how I came by the taste. Father hated cats, mother did not like them, and grandfather and grandmother detested them.'[12] Somehow Daffy won over the strict old lady, giving her solace in her last years:

> Grandmother pets him almost as much as I do. Formerly she did not like my pets and seemed to resent the affection I gave them. But in these lonely later years, neglected by her children, she seems to have changed in this respect and grown fond of the

> Daffies and almost indulgent to them. Well, there
> are many worse friends than the soft, silent, furry,
> cat-folk.[13]

When Grandma MacNeill lay 'in a sort of stupor', taking little interest in anything around her, the 'only living creature she remembered was Daffy, the little gray animal she had petted and which had been her constant company when I had to be away.'[14] Among Grandma's last words were 'Where's Daffy?'[15] Montgomery's love of cats had, in the end, brought her grandmother pleasure.

Grandmother MacNeill died in 1911 and Montgomery then moved briefly to Park Corner, home of her cousins the Campbells. It was this house which was the inspiration for 'Silver Bush' in *Pat of Silver Bush* and *Mistress Pat*. Daffy accompanied her and had to adjust to the resident cats belonging to cousin Frede. One was Mignonette Carissima Montgomery Campbell, who had been grandiosely named by young Maud and Frede (*mignonette* means 'little darling' in French; *carissima* means the same in Italian). Montgomery kept a tuft of Mignonette's fur in a box of treasures for years afterwards. Daffy, transported to Park Corner, never felt fully at home there: 'He was bitterly discontented at first and as wild and frightened as a hare.' He took to disappearing, but somehow always turned up again. He explored the 'the big barn with its mousy straw-loft'[16] and the surrounding woods. But he was never really domesticated at Park Corner.

In July 1911 Montgomery married the Reverend Ewan Macdonald,[17] a Presbyterian minister, in the Park Corner parlour. Ewan had accepted a position at St Paul's Presbyterian Church in Leaskdale, Ontario, so after a honeymoon in Britain the newly-weds settled there. This leaving of her island home was a wrench for Montgomery. One night in England she was suddenly overcome with terrible homesickness. 'I would have dissolved into a fit of crying', she wrote in her journal, 'but one thing saved me. In the hall outside my room I found a pussy cat – a big black pussy cat – a most friendly pussy cat, who allowed me to take her up in my arms and cuddle her. I thought of poor gray Daffy, far, far behind in Canada and I was comforted.'[18]

As soon as she reached her new home, Montgomery sent for Daffy – married life without him couldn't be contemplated. Any house lacking a cat could never be a proper home. So Daffy was shipped from Prince Edward Island and had to endure three miserable days in a crate, arriving on 25 November, dehydrated and scared. But, pampered and caressed, he was soon back to his usual ways – enjoying the freedom of her writing desk, lying on it as she wrote (Montgomery wrote eleven of her twenty-two novels in the Leaskdale Manse), climbing onto the dining table as she ate, curling up on her bed when she slept. Daffy, with the freedom of the entire house and his own special chair in the parlour, was cherished as 'a living link'[19] with her island life.

Daffy was there for comfort when favourite cousin Frede Campbell died suddenly in 1919, and when her husband suffered a breakdown that same year. When Montgomery had her first son, Chester, Daffy adjusted to a child in the house. He solaced her when she had a stillborn birth, and was still a presence in 1915 when her next son, Stuart, arrived. Montgomery's marriage was a troubled one. Ewan suffered from serious depression, something little discussed in that era, especially when the sufferer was a minister supposed to be overseeing the happiness of others. Writing and cats provided a refuge from growing marital misery. When people asked her how she managed to do so much – performing the myriad duties of minister's wife, writing fiction, managing home and servants, and bringing up sons – she claimed that Daffy relaxed her, enabling her to cope.

In 1920 Daffy died. He was accidentally shot when he was fourteen years of age. Montgomery was devastated, but made sure that Daffy had an appropriate farewell:

> We buried him behind the asparagus plot on the lawn – old Daff, with his plumy tail, his distinctive markings, his wild glowing eyes – my old companion of days and nights of long ago, my faithful furry comrade through the many lonely evenings of the past two years. I feel a sense of desolation and loneliness. Ewan says 'Get another cat'. I don't want another cat. No cat can ever again be what Daffy was.[20]

She decided that 'the only real cat is a gray cat'.[21] Daffy had been a true and adored companion.

Of course there were other cats. Pat, also known as Paddy, was officially her sons' cat, but it was Montgomery who truly loved him. And then, on a 1923 visit to Park Corner, she found 'Good Luck', soon known as Lucky, who was silver-grey with black stripes. Lucky had to undergo the same journey Daffy had endured, being shipped to Leaskdale in October. His arrival did not impress Paddy, but eventually a truce was reached. Lucky curled up with her when she read, 'his tiny flanks heaving up and down under my fingers and his little body vibrating with his rapturous purrs'.[22] He greeted her when she came home from outings; he slept on her bed and was demonstrative in a way not typical of cats. 'My only comfort was those two blessed cats – it actually *rested* me to look at those two peaceful unhurried creatures lying on their cushions in ease and grace. It made me feel happy to think that there were really creatures in the world who knew what leisure was … When people ask me what on earth I want to keep two cats for, I tell them I keep them to do my resting for me.'[23]

In 1936 Maud and Ewan left Leaskdale for a parish in Norval. When Paddy died, aged fifteen, he was buried there. In 1935 Ewan's depression grew so severe that he had to resign and the Macdonalds bought a home in Toronto. Montgomery assessed possible purchases according to how cat-friendly they were. Number 210 Riverside Drive, Toronto, was just right: 'I knew I must have the house. What a place for cats to prowl in.'[24] She called it 'Journey's End' (which proved prophetic as it was in this home that Montgomery died on 24 April 1942).

In January 1937 Lucky died from cancer of the liver. For the first day after the event Montgomery was too distraught to plan his burial, but the local builder dug a resting place in the backyard. She had come to see Lucky as 'the only perfect thing I have seen in this world';[25] he was her 'captain of cats', and she missed him horribly. The book she was then working on, *Jane of Lantern Hill*, was a struggle to finish, but was then dedicated 'to the memory of LUCKY, the charming affectionate comrade of fourteen years'.[26] Authors typically turn to words to relieve grief, and Montgomery was no exception. She penned Lucky's obituary in her journal. Consisting of forty handwritten pages, this has been accurately described by Montgomery's biographer Mary Henley Rubio as 'a tour de force in the annals of pet obituaries'.[27] 'Who would have believed', Montgomery asked sadly, 'that the passing of a little cat could leave a house so empty – so desolate?'[28] The ache of longing for Lucky never really left her: 'Cats before him I loved as *cats*. I loved Luck as a human being. And few human beings have given me the happiness he gave me.'[29]

The following year she wrote to her penfriend George MacMillan (their correspondence lasted thirty-nine years) about her departed companion. MacMillan shared her love of cats, so could fully sympathize: 'Nothing in my life, except the death of one dear friend, has caused me more grief and loneliness ... There is rarely a night that, waking, the tears do not come into my eyes when I realize that I cannot put out my hand and feel his silken flank.'[30] Montgomery was at a low ebb psychologically at the time of Lucky's death. Her husband's behaviour was almost unendurable; her eldest son Chester's wildness and academic failures had greatly disappointed her; there had been stressful legal battles with publishers; and there were ongoing problems with servants to contend with. The loss of Lucky, her most reliable source of affection, was a devastating blow from which she never fully recovered.

For Montgomery the affection of a cat was a test of character, and the worthy characters in her fiction all share a love of cats. Readers of her books know there's something wrong with any character who resists feline charm: 'People who don't like cats always seem to think there is some peculiar virtue in not liking them',[31] the heroine *of The Blue Castle* complains. Anne Shirley is adopted by a stray in *Anne of the Island*:

> Trotting along behind her, close to her heels, was quite the most forlorn specimen of the cat-tribe she had ever beheld! The animal was well past kittenhood, lank, thin, disreputable-looking. Pieces of both ears were lacking, one eye was temporarily out of repair, and

one jowl ludicrously swollen. As for colour, if a once
black cat had been well and thoroughly singed the
result would have resembled the hue of this waif's thin,
draggled, unsightly fur.[32]

Anne names him Rusty and comes to love him. She makes
sure, when she leaves Redmond University, that he has a
loving home to go to. In the course of that novel she makes
friends with her suitor's sister, Dorothy Gardner. The
girls bond over a shared love of cats: 'I love them', insists
Dorothy. 'They are so nice and selfish. Dogs are too good
and unselfish. They make me feel uncomfortable. But cats
are gloriously human.'[33] Gilbert Blythe dreams of marrying
Anne and has to propose twice. In his second proposal, he
includes a cat as part of the happiness for which he longs,
telling Anne he dreams of 'a home with a hearth-fire in
it, a cat and dog, the footsteps of friends – and *you*.'[34] Is it
surprising that Anne says Yes to this man, who states that a
cat's purr 'is the most contented sound in the world'?[35]

Emily Byrd Starr, leaving home in *Emily of New Moon*,
is told by aunt Elizabeth Murray to choose *one* of her two
cats before moving to New Moon. Emily prefers Mike, but
chooses Saucy Sal because the family servant, Ellen, prefers
Mike and 'would be good to him'. Emily tells her aunt, 'I
can't live without a cat.' Aunt Elizabeth is having none of it:

> 'Nonsense. There are barn cats at New Moon, but they
> are never allowed in the house.'

'Don't you like cats?' asked Emily wonderingly.
'No, I do not.'
'Don't you like the feel of a nice, soft, fat cat?' persisted Emily.
'No, I would as soon touch a snake.'[36]

All pleading is useless and Emily must steel herself to bid farewell to her beloved Mike.

In *The Blue Castle*, the only one of Montgomery's novels not set on Prince Edward Island, the hero Barney has cats in his wilderness home. In the *Pat* books there are many cats in Judy's kitchen; and Marigold Lesley, heroine of *Magic for Marigold*, holds long conversations with her cats, Lucifer and Witch of Endor. Sara Stanley of *The Story Girl* has Paddy, 'a lordly animal, with a silver-grey coat beautifully marked with darker stripes'.[37] Montgomery wrote in her journals that this Paddy was 'a composite cat, with the characteristics of several pets of mine and the physical attributes of 'Daffy the Second'.[38] Sara introduces herself by announcing 'I am very good friends with all cats. They are so sleek and comfortable and dignified.'[39] Montgomery paid tribute to favourite cats in her fiction.

As a famous writer, L.M. Montgomery was often asked to sign her books for fans. Frequently she added to her signature a small silhouette of a cat. One copy of *Anne's House of Dreams*, held by Toronto's Osborne Collection, shows two little cat silhouettes – a double dose of happiness, a touch of a cat's mysteriousness and suggestiveness, added to Montgomery's authorial signature.

Montgomery's scrapbooks and journals reveal how vital felines were in her life. Photos, jokes about cats, articles and other cat paraphernalia were pasted into the scrapbooks; tufts of cat fur were pressed between pages; while her journals record the antics, personalities and joys of the cats who 'owned' her.

There were many cat friends in L.M. Montgomery's life – Max, Brownie, Topsy, Maggie, Catkin, Pat and Smut. She hoped that, when she died, the spirits of all the cats she'd loved would greet her 'with purrs of gladness at the pearly gates'.[40] But there had been two cats who had meant more to her than the rest, those she most longed to see in whatever afterlife awaited her – Daffy and Lucky. Lucky might have been the one she loved the most, but in my view these cats were misnamed – Daffy should have been called Lucky, for surely to be present at the creation of Canada's greatest novel, to have impeded or assisted in the birth of the immortal Anne, was the most wonderful luck any cat could desire?

PAWS FOR THOUGHT
# Kipling's cat

After his marriage to an American, Rudyard Kipling lived for some years in the little town of Brattleboro in Vermont. One snowy winter's day, as he walked in the woods, he saw a cat walking through the trees, tail aloft. The image impressed itself on his mind, inspiring him to write one of his *Just So Stories* about a cat. *The Cat That Walked by Himself* was first published in 1902 and Kipling included a picture he drew from memory of that cat in the woods.

The story is a 'creation tale', or 'origin story', explaining how, in the Stone Age, a wild cat joined a man, woman and baby in a cave and grew domesticated, catching mice for the cave-dwellers and receiving milk and a place by the fire in return. But Kipling knew enough of cats to understand that they are creatures which will never be fully tamed, in the way that a dog is. At night, his cat continues to roam the woods, 'walking by his wild lone'.[41] The cat refuses to surrender its independence, although it will grace the cave people with its presence in return for food and warmth. Kipling's tale depicts the cat's cunning and intelligence, as well as its strong desire for independence.

Kipling's family did have cats while living in Vermont. His adored daughter Josephine was given a kitten. He wrote the *Just So Stories* after she tragically died in 1899, so the memory of her love for her pet must have been in his mind. But in the story Kipling put much of himself into the character of the cat. He was married to a forceful wife, had children to care for, and was entering a whole new world of domestic responsibilities – there was a part of him still wanting very much to walk 'his wild lone' in the woods of creativity and the imagination.

# NELSON

## who was Chief Mouser to Sir Winston Churchill

*Nelson condescended to live with Sir Winston Churchill, born at Blenheim Palace, Oxfordshire, in 1874, died in London in 1965, statesman, prime minister, soldier, writer who won the 1953 Nobel Prize for Literature.*

Since the days of Cardinal Wolsey, who was comforted by a cat when Lord Chancellor, the seat of English government has needed a cat. The homes of the rich and important were just as plagued by rodents as were the homes of the poor. Number 10 Downing Street, in the heart of London, was no exception. Once it became residence to British prime ministers it also became home to a succession of cats, or 'Chief Mousers' as they were known informally. That title only became official in 2011, when rats were seen scampering across the doorstep in a news report – not a good publicity image. Being 'Chief Mouser' was an important job. But one huge grey cat named Nelson would not have cared whether his title was officially sanctioned or not – Nelson was a law unto himself, and Winston Churchill admired his independence. Nelson was in residence during the crucial years of World War II. In Churchill's view, his cat did a great deal to assist the war effort.

Churchill is today remembered mostly for his political life – twice prime minister, statesman, and leader of Britain during the war. But Churchill was also a writer; in 1953 he won the Nobel Prize for Literature 'for his mastery of historical and biographical description as well as for brilliant oratory in defending exalted human values'. Throughout his long life he published forty-three works in seventy-two volumes – books on war, travel, his father, free trade, himself, social problems, painting, foreign affairs, the Duke of Marlborough, his contemporaries and British history.

Winston Churchill was also an animal lover, and it didn't seem to matter what kind. There are photographs of him patting dogs and goats, cuddling a baby lion and observing goldfish in his pond. As a lonely schoolboy he regularly ended letters home with fond enquiries about favourite pets. Horses were an important part of his soldiering career – he took part in the last cavalry charge at Omdurman; he hunted on horses into his seventies; and in old age he raced thoroughbreds. He worried about a dead badger on the road, bred cows (English Shorthorns) and pigs (Swedish Landrace), kept guinea pigs, swans, goats and, briefly, a pet marmoset. When he kept fowls he struggled to eat them, asserting that it was wrong to eat any animal one had said 'Good morning' to. He owned Charmayne, a ram with a tendency to butt everyone. Churchill defended him as a 'very nice' animal,[1] until the ram knocked him flat – Charmayne was then sold. There was also a parakeet that took nips from his whisky and soda, and in the 1950s he was devoted to Toby, a pet budgerigar that hopped happily over Churchill's desk and accompanied him on travels. Privileged friends found a tiny yellow or green feather tucked into letters from Churchill. In 1961, finding a window open, Toby escaped and was never seen again – his master was devastated.

Throughout his long life he had many dogs and cats as faithful companions (including a tabby named Mickey and a black and white cat called Bob). When Winston died, his cat Jock was said to have been curled up on his bed. Clementine patiently put up with her husband's menagerie at Chartwell and their various London homes, but never shared her husband's passion for animals, unlike their youngest daughter Mary. His children all had particular animal sounds associated with them, while Churchill fondly nicknamed his wife 'Cat' (an indication of his deep love for her). She called him 'Pug'.

It was on Whitehall, a historic London street, that the first encounter between Churchill and feline Nelson occurred. From September 1939 to May 1940 Churchill served as First Lord of the Admiralty and was also a member of the War Cabinet. Admiralty House stands on Whitehall. Outside the building, one day in 1940, Churchill stopped to watch a pursuit – a large grey tom was chasing a huge dog. Much impressed by the cat's bravery, he took him home and christened him Nelson, in honour of the great admiral of Trafalgar. Winston rapidly grew devoted to his new pet.

Within months, Churchill was elected prime minister and moved into 10 Downing Street, historic residence of British leaders. Neville Chamberlain moved out, but left behind his cat to continue catching mice there. Churchill derisively called Chamberlain's cat 'the Munich Mouser', a reference to the failed peace attempt that was Chamberlain's mission to Munich. When Nelson arrived on the scene, 'the Munich Mouser' was on the receiving end of Nelson's fighting spirit. Newspapers reported the feud and speculated as to which animal would win the day. 'The Munich Mouser' decided that his best political move would be to find a new home as fast as possible, leaving Nelson victor of the field. 'The Munich Mouser' died in July 1943 at the Foreign Office. Anthony Eden remarked: 'Winston says that he died of remorse, and chose his death bed accordingly.'[2]

Nelson was not the only cat in residence at number 10. Tango, a marmalade cat ('beautiful and richly-marked' according to Mary Churchill), came with the family when they moved in. Tango (also known as 'Mr Cat') had originally been a nursery cat, bought to amuse the children, but he soon found that adults had more to offer (Churchill fed Tango choice pieces of mutton). Strangely, Churchill persisted in referring to Tango, a neutered male, as 'she'. Tango lived at Chartwell before the war (they bought the home in 1924), but that house was closed during the war, so he had to move with the family. Tango was once painted by Sir William Nicholson, a distinguished artist of the day. Tango died in 1942 and Clementine insisted the bad news be kept from her husband. It was the week when Tobruk fell, the war was going badly for the Allies, and she feared the news about his beloved cat might be too much for Winston.

Smoky succeeded Tango, arriving in 1943. He was grey, of uncertain lineage but probably with a touch of Persian. He'd wait outside the bedroom, wanting to share Churchill's breakfast inside. However, Smoky was a moody cat, and his attacks on legs and expensive stockings made him highly unpopular with visiting secretaries. Clementine, writing to her husband when he was in Casablanca, told him 'Smoky wanders about disconsolate'[3] – all his cats loved Winston. It was Smoky who shared VE Day with his master, contentedly curling up on Winston's lap, surely sensing his relief, and both feeling that a huge task was over.

Nelson settled in to the prime ministerial residence and made himself completely at home. It was rumoured that he sometimes sat in on wartime cabinet meetings. Churchill kept a dining-room chair free for Nelson near his own and fed him titbits of salmon when Clementine wasn't looking. Caressing Nelson's ears, he chatted happily to his cat about politics. There was always a place for Nelson on Winston's lap. As with his other cats, he called Nelson 'Darling'. But there was at least one occasion when Nelson failed to live up to the courage of his namesake. During one German air raid, Nelson scurried under a bed. 'Nelson, summon the spirit of the tiger', exhorted Churchill. 'Think of your namesake. No one named Nelson slinks under the bed in a time of crisis.'[4] Nelson emerged, but another siren sent him scurrying back to his haven. In 1940, during the height of the Blitz, Churchill wrote a memo: 'Pray let six new offices be fitted out for my use ... I will inform you at six each evening at which office I shall dine, work and sleep. Accommodation will be required for Mrs Churchill, two shorthand typists, three secretaries, and Nelson.'[5]

Nelson was an extremely fortunate cat. He was likely a stray when Winston met him, and London during World War II was not a good time to be a cat, homeless or otherwise. In 1939, when war had just started and regulations were being frantically issued to ensure people learned quickly what to expect, a formal memo was issued suggesting that domestic dogs and cats be put down. Rationing was to be introduced, food would be scarce, so government warned Londoners that it could be traumatic to watch Fido or Puss starve. Far better to have them euthanized at once! As a result, some people sent their pets into the country, but many patriotically took their pets to the vet, or to mobile vans that were doing the gruesome job. It is thought today that about 750,000 dogs and cats were killed in what became known as 'The Great British Pet Massacre'. The 'Waste of Food Order', passed by the government in August, 1940, insisted that good food must not be fed to pets. In September 1940 the bombings restarted. Owners rushed to have pets put down, aware that animals were traumatised by the raids (some vets made up special tranquillizing mixtures to calm distressed cats). People were also concerned that, if home was bombed, a territorial cat would simply hang around the bomb site, hungry. Later, when the British settled into life at war, many regretted killing cats and blamed the government for whipping up anti-pet hysteria unnecessarily.[6]

However, there were strict regulations about food for animals and no ration coupons for pets. 'Chappie', a large pet-food factory in Slough, was closed. Milk was rationed for everyone in 1941. Before the war Churchill had given his cats fresh cream (if no saucer was handy, he simply poured cream onto the table and invited his cats to lap it up), but as a wartime cat Nelson went without cream. By 1942 serious food shortages resulted in an increase in cat thefts in Britain. Stolen cats were killed, for their meat and fur.

Cats did, however, have an important role to play throughout the war. Rodents flourished in bomb sites, and in grain stores and places where food reserves were held. Backyard poultry and rabbit-keeping also attracted rats and mice. The vermin needed to be exterminated. Londoners were asked to donate cats to places where such stores were located. Cats employed in stores and factories were allowed special food rations and a portion of milk powder (but only of damaged packages deemed unfit for human consumption). Cats were kept as mascots on ships (Churchill, visiting HMS *Prince of Wales*, paused to stroke a black cat on deck. The cat, 'Blackie', was promptly renamed 'Churchill' in his honour and survived a Japanese attack on the ship. Blackie was last heard of disembarking in Singapore, where he disappeared, no doubt meeting a grisly fate). Cats were kept in barracks, air bases and military field offices – there providing stress relief for men living in extremely tense situations. Cats were also used as an early form of siren warning. Their acute hearing could pick up a siren before a human ear could – those extra precious minutes could save lives.

Churchill told a colleague one day that Nelson was assisting the war effort by acting as prime ministerial hot-water bottle, thus saving on the fuel needed to heat water for a real one. Nelson also provided stress-relief and time-out for Churchill during his incredibly challenging job. Nelson was 'Chief Mouser' from 1940 to 1946. After

Churchill left Number 10, standards for resident cats deteriorated and salmon and other delicacies were no longer on the feline menu. In 1948 a member of staff, Mrs Law, wrote a note asking for the office cats' food money to be increased, as she found it impossible to buy a week's food for 1/6d.

Churchill would have loved to spend more time with one very different cat – a lion cub which was a 1943 gift from London Zoo in celebration of British victories in North Africa. The lion has been ubiquitous in British heraldry for centuries – the association of the King of Beasts with Churchill's 'roars' (speeches) and strong leadership was inevitable. He was delighted with his new pet: 'I shall have much pleasure in becoming the possessor of the lion.' Regretfully, Churchill had to hand the cub back: 'I do not want the lion at the moment either at Downing Street or at Chequers, owing to the Ministerial calm which prevails there. But the Zoo is not far away, and situations may arise in which I shall have great need of it.'[7] He did visit the lion, named Rota, at the zoo. Rota died in 1955, after siring sixty cubs. He was stuffed and is now on display at a museum in Florida. When Churchill was once asked which animal he'd have loved to be, the answer was a tiger. He adored big cats, as well as small ones.

It is not known when Nelson's mousing career was ended by death. He was replaced by other cats – Margate arrived in 1953 (Churchill had just given an important speech in the town); Whisky wandered in one day, stayed some years, and then mysteriously left; and then there was Jock – this marmalade cat with white chest and paws was given to Churchill as an 88th birthday present by his private secretary Sir John (Jock) Colville. Jock the cat liked to escort Churchill into the drawing room, always two stately paces ahead. Churchill took Jock to his London home at Hyde Park Gate when travelling there from Chartwell. Jock, who was with Churchill when he died in 1965, lived on until 1975 and died aged thirteen. He was buried in Chartwell's pet cemetery. Chartwell is now run by the National Trust, but Winston's family requested that a cat should always be in residence. Ever since, there has been a marmalade cat named Jock at Chartwell. In 2020 Jock VII arrived (a six-month-old rescue cat). He has made himself completely at home, finding sunny corners of the beautiful garden in which to cat-nap, chasing butterflies, and sometimes welcoming visitors to the historic property. Jock VII receives fan mail and has an internet presence – Winston Churchill would surely have approved.

And Nelson has been succeeded by many other cats as 'Chief Mouser'. In 1929 the Treasury authorized spending a penny a day from petty cash towards the maintenance of an efficient cat (today the upkeep is paid by the prime minister, rather than the taxpayer). The current 'Chief Mouser' is Larry (a brown and white tabby from Battersea, who once engaged in fierce rivalry with Palmerston, the Foreign

Office cat next door), but he is now too old and staid to fight. Larry has served under six prime ministers. Peter III served five and enjoyed a starring role on BBC TV in the *Tonight* programme. There has also been Humphrey (named after the civil servant in *Yes, Minister*), a stray who refused to eat any cat food but Whiskas. Humphrey had to move out after the Blairs moved in, as Cherie Blair reportedly detested cats. Other Whitehall mousers have included Gladstone, Evie, Ossie and Wilberforce. Number 10 currently has three feline residents, as Larry has been joined by the Starmer family's Jojo and the grandly named Siberian cat Prince.

There is some debate as to how many rodents any 'Chief Mouser' has actually caught (Larry was spotted in an altercation with a fox, while Humphrey was accused of savaging a duck in St James Park), but probably the mere presence of a cat is enough to deter vermin. 'Paw patrol' in this seat of British political power is alive and well.

PAWS FOR THOUGHT
## Library cats

Cats and books seem to belong together, like bacon and eggs, or wine and cheese. Medieval monks knew that a cat in the monastery library would deter rats from nibbling valuable manuscripts, candles and anything else within reach. In the eighteenth century Russian Empress Elizabeth ordered cats to be transported to her Winter Palace library so they could kill the rats there. Many modern libraries have welcomed cats into their bookish domains. In 1987 an official Library Cat Society (now defunct) was created in the USA to encourage the establishing and recognition of library cats.

There are many positives to keeping a cat in a library. Cats befriend patrons, boost the morale of librarians, help encourage literacy in the young, and generate publicity for their libraries, especially on social media. Libraries have traditionally encouraged silence, and cats are quiet creatures, as well as low maintenance.

Not everyone likes the idea, however. People with pet allergies detest cats in public buildings, while others complain that their 'service animals' (such as guide dogs) dislike encountering library cats. But when the Putnam Valley Library of New York removed the cat from its institution, the local community was decidedly upset. Two future benefactors deleted the library from their wills.

Contemporary library cats have featured in film and literature. The most famous is the appropriately named Dewey (his full name was Dewey Readmore Books), who lived for nineteen years in Iowa's Spencer Library. Orange Dewey was dumped in a book-return bin, but was rapidly embraced by library staff and the public, and spent the rest of his life promoting reading. Books were published about Dewey, who died in 2006. The 1997 film *Puss in Books: The Adventures of a Library Cat* was a charming movie about various library cats around America. The cats featured had delightful titles – The Boss, Librarian in Charge of

Rodent Control, Marketing and Public Relations Manager, Library Mascot and Library King. Some library cats have wonderfully bookish names: Stacks, Pages, Browser, Libris, Bibliocat and Homer are some examples. In Oxford, Christ Church cats Alice (named for Lewis Carroll's heroine) and Meadow have Bodleian Library cards, while Hertford College's Simpkin (one of four Simpkins named for *The Tailor of Gloucester*) battles with Walter, the cat Exeter College named after its founder. These Oxford felines have free run of their college libraries.

Cats welcomed into a library prefer managerial roles and like to have their status officially recognized. The job requires no training, while salaries come in the form of regular meals and lots of attention.

# BOISE
## who was a Christmas treat for Ernest Hemingway

*Boise condescended to live with Ernest Hemingway, born in Illinois, USA, 1899, died in Idaho, 1961, novelist, short-story writer and journalist, winner of the 1954 Nobel Prize for Literature.*

It was Christmas morning in 1942 when a skinny black and white kitten wandered into a bar in the fishing village of Cojimar, 10 miles from Havana, in Cuba. He was hungry and hoping for scraps. La Terraza, the bar, was fairly quiet – locals had been partying the night before and were sleeping off their excesses. One man was there with his two young sons, Gregory and Patrick. The waiter brought the trio a dish of fresh prawns and they all tucked in. But that man, known around the world for his macho huntin', shootin' and fishin', was a complete softie when it came to cats. When the scrawny kitten rubbed against his leg, he reached down and fed the poor thing a prawn. The kitten wolfed that down, growling with pleasure. The man asked the bar owner who owned the poor waif. He was always enraged by cruelty to animals – perhaps he planned to have words with the cat's owner about a better food supply for his pet. But the barman replied that, to his knowledge, the kitten was homeless, and suggested that the diner take him home. The customer protested that he had two cats at home already.

It only took a few minutes for the bar owner to insist that a bit of 'Cojimar' blood would be good for the cats this customer already owned, and for Patrick and Gregory to urge their dad to rescue the creature, and the deed was done. That kitten had just had the luckiest encounter of its life, the man had found a friend and 'brother' in the kitten, and literature would be enriched. For the man was Ernest Hemingway and the kitten was Boise, the cat that Hemingway came to love more than any other and the one he immortalized in thirty-five pages of a novel. The kitten was taken to the Finca Vigia, Hemingway's Cuban farm, there to begin a life of pampered ease. Hemingway had just had the best Christmas treat ever.

The kitten did not start life as Boise; he was first named Dillinger. But Hemingway believed in changing the names of his cats according to their developing personalities or his own moods. Dillinger was soon Dingie, then he was Boy, Boysy and even Boissy D'Angelas, before the Hemingways settled on Boise. Boise was the name of a cruising warship in which Hemingway took an interest (the naval vessel had been named Boise for Idaho's state capital).

Boise met two other cats when he arrived at the farm. Princessa, an elegant Persian, had been purchased by Hemingway at a cattery in Miami. She was smoke grey, with golden eyes and excellent manners, a very dignified animal. She rose when Hemingway did, stretched out on his desk while he wrote, and knew exactly who was boss in his house. Worried that Princessa might be lonely, Hemingway had then adopted Willy (also known as Mr Willy or Uncle Willy), a grey and black striped half-Maltese, who was especially fond of the catnip that grew near the house. Hemingway hoped that Willy would prove a suitor to Princessa, as he was keen to experiment with mating his pets to create new feline breeds. Soon after Boise's arrival, Good Will, an Angora, also joined the cat clan.

Boise settled in quickly. He was a striking-looking kitten, with 'his handsome black and white markings, his white chest and forelegs and the black, like a formal mask across his eyes and forehead'.[1] Soon he was accompanying the famous writer on his daily walks, ambling by his side on Cuban roads. He shared Hemingway's bed, along with Martha, Hemingway's third wife, who also adored cats. When Hemingway couldn't sleep, he told Boise stories of other cats he'd loved, and during the day he tried to teach Boise circus tricks. As a boy Ernest had loved the circus – wanting to recreate its magic, he trained his cats to make a cat pyramid just as the circus lions did. He was eager to take Boise on his beloved boat, the *Pilar*, but Boise protested at this – dry land was the only place for a self-respecting cat. 'Cats don't want to be pals', Hemingway once insisted; 'they must be kings and queens.'[2] Boise rapidly became king of Hemingway's domain.

Gregory and Patrick (children of Hemingway's second marriage with Pauline Pfeiffer) were only with their father for holidays. They played with Boise while there, and were often photographed by their father with the new kitten. When they returned to their mother, Hemingway had his cat to himself. He sent regular letters to his sons about Boise's activities, knowing they would be missing the kitten.

'One cat just leads to another',[3] Hemingway wrote to his first wife Hadley the following year – at that time he had eleven cats. It was certainly the case that cats rapidly followed each other at the Cuban home. Martha soon had Thruster, her favourite, and a companion as she too tried writing a novel. By 1945 the Hemingways had twenty-three cats on the property, along with five dogs. Princessa had taken a liking to Boise, and before long the pair produced kittens (Martha's Thruster was one of Boise's sons). Friendless, Friendless's Brother, Furhouse and Fatso were more products of that union. Thruster had three kittens: Spendthrift (he became Spendy, but his original name was Stephen Spender, after the poet), Shakespeare (this was changed to Barbershop, then Shopsky) and Ecstasy.

The cats were given the run of Finca Vigia, and as their number grew Martha became concerned. The males sprayed urine to mark their territory, and the mating was becoming incestuous. Boise mated with his daughter Thruster and she produced two blind kittens (both named Blindie, they survived thanks to Hemingway's tender care). While her husband was away on a trip, Martha took matters into her own hands and called in a local vet to sterilize all those cats old enough to be fixed. Hemingway was furious – 'she cut my cats',[4] he stated bitterly upon his return. What especially upset him was that Boise was among those neutered – there were no more love sessions with Princessa or his daughters after that. Without his masculinity, Boise grew more laid back, spending more time at Hemingway's side or on the windowsill near his desk.

All Hemingway's four wives loved cats – he'd probably never have married them had they been cat-phobic.

Whether Martha's 'crime' in sterilizing his beloved pets was the last nail in the coffin of their marriage is not known, but she was soon replaced by fourth wife Mary Welsh. All his wives, except Pauline, heard cat-related terms of endearment from Hemingway – Kitten, Kittner, Katherine Cat, Kitty, Kat and Feather Kitty were all nicknames he gave the women he loved. Martha had reciprocated by calling him 'Big Kitten' when feeling especially loving. Catherine was his favourite name for a woman because it started with 'Cat' – he gave it to two of his heroines, Catherine Bourne in *The Garden of Eden* and Catherine Barkley in *A Farewell to Arms*.

Work and adventure often called Hemingway from home, and every time he departed Boise fretted. An opened suitcase disturbed him. *Islands in the Stream*, the book in which Boise features so heavily, gives a description of this anxiety (in the novel, Boise's alter ego is also Boise): 'Boise was following him, a little worried at this going away but not panicking since there was no baggage and no packing.'[5] When absent, Hemingway often sent kisses to the 'cotsies'.

Boise was an unusual eater and loved to join Hemingway at the table and share his food: welcome at every meal, and hand-fed, Boise ate mangos, chilli con carne, coleslaw, pies, cakes and chop suey. He was also served salmon, turtle, various meats and milk (fresh from the farm's cows). Most of the other cats were cared for by René Villarreal, the Finca Vigia caretaker. Their dinner time must have been quite a sight: 'The place is so damned big it doesn't really seem as though there were many cats until you see them all moving like a mass migration at feeding time.'[6] Hemingway's fondness for alcohol was legendary – he taught some of his cats to drink whiskey and milk with him (Friendless grew positively alcoholic). Keeping so many pets was costly – Hemingway mentioned the cases of salmon that had to be purchased. When he won the Nobel Prize for Literature, a considerable part of his $35,000 cheque went on cat food.

Mary Hemingway, the new wife in residence, loved Boise, who returned her affection. To show his esteem, he brought her fruit rats, usually still half alive. 'Boise leaped in. He had two fruit rats in his mouth'[7] and he proceeded to play with them on the bed (again, this is described in *Islands in the Stream*). Mary knew the gifts were meant as a compliment, but the fruit rats were too much. She attempted to get the cats out of the house. Hemingway took some persuading because he didn't want his cats' feelings to be hurt, but finally gave in to Mary's wishes. A cat tower was built, which still stands there today (and is still enjoyed by cats). The tower was 40 feet high, had a patio on the roof (where Mary sunbathed nude) and an outside staircase. 'It ought to be almost part of the house', Hemingway insisted, 'so cotsies do not feel sent to Siberia or abandoned.'[8] The room especially dedicated as the cat mansion was on the second floor and Hemingway made a workroom for himself on the fourth floor, but when he found that his animals disdained to visit him there he moved back into the house where the study and bathroom windows faced the tower, so he could see the cats as he wrote or trimmed his beard. However, Boise did *not* have to go to the tower or suffer any form of banishment – as top favourite, he continued to have full run of the house. His scratching pole remained exactly where it had always stood – indoors.

By 1954 Mary and Ernest Hemingway had fifty-four cats at Finca Vigia. Hemingway could identify and name each one. By his bed was the useful *The Care and Handling of Cats: A Manual for Modern Cat Owners* by Doris Bryant, published in 1944. All were looked after by René when the Hemingways travelled. In 1959 Hemingway purchased a property in Idaho and began going there for extended periods – soon he had cats at that Ketchum house as well. He rescued kittens he found in an old barn, and it was in Idaho that he acquired his favourite dog, Black Dog. When he took this new pet back to Cuba, his biggest worry was Boise's probable reaction to a canine intruder, but Boise and Black Dog were soon best friends.

For Ernest Hemingway a house was just not a home if it lacked cats. They'd always been an important part of his life. He'd had cats as a boy (his father, Clarence, although a doctor, had initially considered being a vet and often performed medical procedures on sick neighbourhood animals). From childhood, Ernest had loved to study animals – their habitats, migration patterns and hunting behaviour. Horribly, as he grew older, he often killed the animals he studied – shooting birds, then lions and other magnificent big cats. But he fortunately lost this desire to kill, and simply admired and studied big game as he aged and mellowed. As a boy, Ernest often rescued strays. A family holiday to Walloon Lake involved taking Catherine Tiger cat and her kittens along on the train. His first love interest, Agnes von Kurowsky, once wrote to him about rescuing a kitten – how could he *not* fall in love with her when she did such things. His early writings featured cats too – his short story 'Cat in the Rain' is about a lonely woman who tries to rescue a kitten in a downpour.

In Paris Ernest and first wife Hadley were desperately poor and couldn't afford to feed a cat. They had to make do with Parisian café cats near their apartment. However, when their son John (always known as Bumby) was very young a friend gave them a cat. This was Feather Puss (or F. Puss). He became chief babysitter, as Hemingway recorded in his Paris memoir *A Moveable Feast*: 'F. Puss lay beside Bumby in the tall cage bed and watched the door with his big yellow eyes, and would let no one come near him when we were out.'[9] F. Puss was his companion as Hemingway worked on his first book.

Over the next years, in spite of an unsettled lifestyle, Hemingway frequently managed to find space for a cat. Their names were many and various – Sir Winston Churchill, Pony, Taskforce, Bates, Mooky, Pelusa, Stranger, Clark Gable, Zane Grey and Littless Kitty (also known as Nuisance Value, whose purr was like a loud blast) were some of them.

In 1928 Hemingway and his second wife Pauline went to live in Florida's Key West. His home there is today a museum. The town was sometimes known as 'the Isle of Cats' because of its large population of strays, drawn there by fishermen and the scraps they dropped. It was in 1931 that he and Pauline moved into the Key West house on Whitehead Street, the first home Hemingway owned. Cats roamed the property. He loved teaching them tricks, as he reported in a 1943 letter to ex-wife Hadley: 'I have taught Uncle Wolfer, Dillinger and Will to walk along the railings to the top of the porch pillars and make a pyramid like lions and have taught Friendless to drink with me (whiskey and milk).'[10]

It was in Florida that Hemingway acquired his most unusual cat, the gift of a sea captain friend, Stanley Dexter. The cat was a white one, named Snowball, and was unusual because he was a six-toed, or polydactyl, cat. This abnormality is not due to any genetic fault; rather, the cause lies in a faulty region of DNA that acts as a control switch, normally turning a gene on at the right time in the right place to direct the formation of fingers and toes as a baby or kitten develops in the womb. Hemingway's cat effectively had a faulty switch, and so had six toes. This defect was particularly common on the eastern seaboard of the USA. Cats with extra toes were popular with sailors who thought they brought a ship luck and were better mousers; they also believed that an added toe prevented the animal from sliding off the deck too easily – such cats can use the extra toe almost as humans use a thumb. Usually, the extra digit is on the front paws, but there are cases where all four paws are so endowed. A normal cat has eighteen toes, five on each front paw and four on each back one. Polydactyls can have as many as seven toes per paw – the polydactyl record holder is Jake, who boasted twenty-eight toes.[11] Hemingway's caretaker Gene noted that 'some of the cats' feet had so many toes that the cats looked like they were walking on dog feet.'[12]

Snowball passed his extra toes on to his offspring (the first of whom was Snow White), and soon the Key West property was thronged with many-toed cats. Today more than sixty cats call the place home (still sleeping on Hemingway's bed) and about half of them have six toes (such cats are now often known as 'Hemingway Cats'). They are fed twice daily. Hemingway always longed for a daughter, but when no baby girl arrived he found solace in his cats: 'Since I've spent so much time with my cats and seen everything they have to go through, I don't mind so much never having a daughter.'[13] He built a catwalk, so his animals could climb from the balcony to his writer's studio (where he worked on *Death in the Afternoon*, *Green Hills of Africa*, *To Have and Have Not* and *The Snows of Kilimanjaro*). He even turned an old urinal (brought home after a drunken binge at Sloppy Joe's bar) into a cat's fountain – it's still there too. And there was a cat cemetery for when they needed burial. Today many of his Key West cats have individual tombstones – Marilyn Monroe, Errol Flynn and Fred Astaire, for example.

The large number of cats at Finca Vigia (at one time there were fifty-seven) was not something new in Hemingway's life – cats were eternally important to him, and his admiration for the species never waned. He loved their emotional honesty: 'Male or female, a cat will show you how it feels about you. People hide their feelings for various reasons, but cats never do.'[14] His feline friends gave him not only honesty but solace. Stroking a cat comforted him as he struggled with illness and depression, and he insisted that they helped him in his work, providing valuable aid in his writing of novels. He would have agreed with the French vet Dr Fernand Méry (author of *The Life, History and Magic of the Cat*), who stated that 'cats are the natural companions of intellectuals'.[15] They were Hemingway's 'purr factories', his 'love sponges', and they gave him love and devotion, which he invariably requited.[16]

But even with their legendary nine lives, cats do die, and Hemingway began to worry about his adored Boise. Princessa died in 1950, lying on a pile of his clothes, then

Willy was hit by a car soon afterwards. Hemingway kept a logbook recording the births and deaths of all his cats, and hated having to make sad notations. In 1953 he went on a final safari in Africa – leaving Boise was terrible, for he was frail and old and had to be lifted on to Hemingway's stomach where he would curl up and sleep. Boise was inconsolable when he sensed Hemingway was leaving. For his own sake, he needed to be locked away so he couldn't see departure preparations. Hemingway came home from that trip a seriously damaged man – a flying accident had left his body broken and bruised. Boise was there to keep him company through the months of recovery. 'The way he and Boise felt now, he thought, neither one wanted to outlive the other'[17] is how Hemingway described the situation in *Islands in the Stream*.

In 1955 Boise suffered a heart attack, but did recover. The following year Hemingway had, reluctantly, to travel to Peru. Boise, the cat he called 'my Brother', died in his absence. He was fourteen. Upon his return, Hemingway wrote to a friend, Gianfranco Ivancich: 'Boise died while we were away. I was very sorry not to be with him when he died. He died in the night and did not suffer at all. It was a heart attack and we buried him along side of Willie … Letters about the death of animals are not the best to send.'[18] Boise's grave is by the back terrace, marked with a half circle of stones. Hemingway was convinced that one day he and Boise would be reunited in heaven.

Hemingway's Cuban days were nearly over, with revolution making the place dangerous. He still enjoyed his cats – Cristóbal, a tiger cat, was his next 'important cat', along with Izzy the Cat, but they never came close to taking Boise's place in his heart. Cristóbal loved eating corn on the cob from Hemingway's hand. In 1957 Black Dog died and Hemingway grew seriously depressed. When he and Mary left Cuba in a hurry, the situation becoming threatening, caretaker René was paid to keep caring for the cats they had to leave behind.

In Idaho he had Big Boy Peterson, a solid, trusting cat. But by now Hemingway's depression and illnesses were so great that life, even with cats, no longer seemed worth living. On the night of 1 July 1961 Hemingway said to his wife 'Good night, my kitten.'[19] 'Kitten' was the last word he spoke. Early the next morning he shot himself. Big Boy Peterson was at his side.

Hemingway's widow was contacted by the Cuban government about the farm near Havana. His papers, books and possessions were all still there, along with his cats. Fidel Castro was a fan of Hemingway's books; when he visited Finca Vigía, all the cats trotted around after him as he made a tour of inspection. Mary was permitted to visit the property and arrange shipment of some items (papers and books went to Boston's John F. Kennedy Library). Mary found the cats thinner. She left money for the staff there, but not for the cats, and over the next years they wandered away in search of food and homes. Today the house remembers Hemingway's love of cats in an appropriate way – they tend three cats there. Hemingway is not there to name them, call for them, stroke them, and generally give them the sort of five-star treatment cats know they deserve, but at least felines still roam the property.

His 'top cat' Boise was granted literary fame. Hemingway put Boise, without any name change, straight into *Islands in the Stream*. Thirty-five pages describe Boise, praise Boise and delight in Boise. He began the novel in 1950 but it was only published posthumously, in 1970. Thomas Hudson, Hemingway's fictional alter ego, drinks heavily and fights depression. But Hudson loves cats, and his felines are Princessa, Goats and Boise. Cats comfort him when he mourns his dead son; cats amuse him by gifting fruit rats; cats sleep by his side and share his chair. Hudson is more comfortable with cats than with people. Few cats have been given such fine literary tributes as the one Ernest Hemingway gave his beloved Boise.

## PAWS FOR THOUGHT
## The literary cats of Harry Potter

In the first volume of the *Harry Potter* series, readers meet a cat. Her name is Mrs Norris and she belongs to the Hogwarts caretaker, Argus Filch. Mrs Norris has a very strong connection to her master, immediately alerting him to any student misbehaviour within the castle. Mrs Norris is not an attractive animal, with her skeletal body, dusty fur and bulging yellow lamp-like eyes that see what others would prefer her not to see. In *Harry Potter and the Chamber of Secrets* Mrs Norris is petrified by the Serpent of Slytherin (in the film version of the book no real cat was used for this gruesome scene), and has to be revived by a magic potion.

Mrs Norris is wonderfully named for a character in Jane Austen's *Mansfield Park*. Mrs Norris in that novel is disagreeable, judgemental and always seems to be where she is least wanted. J.K. Rowling has stated that Jane Austen is one of her favourite authors, so the naming of Filch's cat is a quirky tribute to a writer whose works have given her great pleasure.

In the film versions of the *Harry Potter* novels, three different cat 'actors' took on the role of Mrs Norris – Maximus, Alanis and Cornelius, all of them Maine Coon cats.

Crookshanks is the other cat in the series. He is purchased as a pet by Hermione Granger. He is a half-Kneazle ginger animal, not much liked by her friends Harry and Ron. Hermione is the first person to show him empathy and he finally rewards her loyalty in the last book in the series. Crookshanks has a squashed face and a large furry tail and has a remarkable ability to solve problems on his own. His name comes from the Scottish 'cruikshanks', meaning bandy-legged. Possibly J.K. Rowling chose the name as a tribute to Scotland, the country where she chose to make her home.

# OLD TIMER
## who gained Margaret Mitchell's sympathies

*Old Timer condescended to live with
Margaret Mitchell, born in Atlanta, Georgia,
in 1900, died in Atlanta in 1949, journalist and
author of the bestselling Gone with the Wind.*

When Margaret Mitchell was three years old, her parents, Eugene and Maybelle Mitchell, decided they would like a nice photograph of their only daughter. In 1903 few people had their own cameras (the Kodak camera had been first offered for sale in America in 1888) and so a visit to a portrait photographer was necessary. Unfortunately, Margaret, who even at that young age had a determination all her own, refused to cooperate. She cried and wriggled off the chair in which the photographer had placed her. Probably the long-suffering photographer had coped with infant tantrums before, and he offered what proved to be the perfect solution to the problem. He produced a kitten. Once Margaret had been persuaded that the desired photo was of the pussy cat, and not of her own infant self, she cooperated happily. Posing with puss on her lap, she was delighted to be a feline assistant, and the photographer could get to work. Legs dangling, frilled white skirts around her knees, hair curled and tidy, Margaret Mitchell posed the kitten with pleasure, clutching it in her arms. The kitten looks somewhat astonished at being so firmly held, but it cooperated long enough for the photographer to finish the job. It wouldn't be the last time that this woman, who came to detest publicity and press photographers, would hold a cat in her arms to ease the discomfort of being photographed.

Margaret Mitchell was born in Atlanta, Georgia, in November 1900, into a society not that far removed from the one she would describe in her only, world-famous, novel, *Gone with the Wind*.[1] Young white women of good families were expected to always remember they were ladies – they should be beautiful and demure debutantes, marry well, then settle down to become respectable wives and mothers. Mitchell, like her heroine Scarlett O'Hara, never fitted that mould. The name she preferred to be known by was Peggy. A tomboy, she liked to wear boys' clothes, climb trees, ride her pony in daredevil escapades, and use bad language. 'At the age of six', she recalled, 'I was not concerned about being a lady.'[2] Stories of the American Civil War enchanted her. The burning of Atlanta, Sherman's 'march to the south', the battles and the patriotism of Southerners, were all familiar to her from an early age. Entranced, she sat on the veranda of her beloved grandmother's home, listening to such tales. Strangely, no one ever thought to tell the child that the South had actually *lost* the war – when she finally discovered that inconvenient fact, at the age of ten, it came as a terrible shock.

Stories were one passion of Mitchell's childhood. The other was animals – she adored them. Pet ducks (Mr and Mrs Drake), horses and ponies, a cow, dogs (there was a Collie named Colonel), turtles and even two alligators (presumably very juvenile ones) were all members of her menagerie. She played 'mother' to many kittens and cats in her youth, while her real mother was patiently long-suffering about her daughter's pet addiction. Mitchell was a shy child who felt more comfortable with animals than with the human beings who, her mother insisted, must always be treated with true Southern politeness. Cats all had a part to play in her imaginative world. When a tree house was built for her, she took them up there with her by ingenious methods, despite their protests. One of her cats, Piedy (one assumes she was so named because of a pied coat), was taken up into the boughs, and her kittens were hoisted up to the tree hut as well. After Piedy, she had the fabulously named cats Hypatia and Lowpatia. Leisure hours were devoted to teaching Lowpatia how to 'salute' with his right paw behind his ear. Mitchell was very proud of her pet's trick. After the publication of her book, her brother Stephens recalled that he never saw her play with dolls. However, like her mother Maybelle, she loved cats and kittens and had lots of them.

Soon she was writing stories about animals. These were illustrated by the young author, bound together in covers of her design, and then published under her very own company, 'Urchin Publishing Company'. Peggy was usually the heroine of these tales, riding fast on her ponies and committing acts of incredible bravery. Encouraged by a teacher at school, she continued to write stories of adventure and heroism throughout her childhood.

Peggy Mitchell went off to university but lasted only one year at prestigious Smith College. Although her writing was praised by an English professor, she felt she did not fit in with the other girls; and the early death of her mother (Maybelle died in the Spanish Flu epidemic) and her father's need for his daughter at home, resulted in her leaving without a degree. She dreamed of being a journalist — not a career that was usual for Southern women at the time.

She was petite, vivacious and unusual, and men were drawn to her like moths to a candle. In 1922, against her family's wishes, she married one of them — Berrien 'Red' Upshaw. It was a disaster: Red was a violent drunk, and after only a few months the pair separated. In July 1925 she married John Marsh — he had been Red's best man at the wedding, but had adored Peggy from the first moment he saw her. Mr and Mrs Marsh settled into an Atlanta apartment, affectionately called 'the Dump' – it is today the Margaret Mitchell House and Museum. Peggy secured a job on *The Atlanta Journal*, where she more than held her own among the male journalists. She loved interviewing the famous, reporting on Georgia's history and exploring topics connected with the modern Southern woman. One of her colleagues, the humourist Don Marquis, wrote poems and sketches about a disreputable alley-cat, Mehitabel (actually always presented as 'mehitabel', as Marquis couldn't locate the shift key to create capitals). These appeared in *The Atlanta Journal*. Margaret and John loved reading about Mehitabel's antics.

She resigned from her reporting job in 1926. A serious ankle injury kept her housebound for months. John struggled to bring home enough library books to keep her occupied. Frustrated, he suggested she write a book of her own, instead of reading so many written by other people. The rest, as they say, is history. *Gone with the Wind* began to emerge in parts, never written sequentially. Once a section of the book was finished, the wad of manuscript was stuffed in a cupboard, or used to prop up a wobbly couch, or pushed under the bed. Pansy O'Hara (as her heroine was initially named) began to occupy more and more of Mitchell's thoughts. Her lifelong fascination with the Civil War gave shape and background to the dramatic story, while Scarlett's hopeless love for Ashley and her deep connection with her home, Tara, drove this feisty heroine to save herself and her family from the ruination in the South. *Gone with the Wind* was published in 1936 and was an instant international bestseller. Mitchell was exhausted by the effort of finishing it and surviving the publication process, and decided that she would never write another novel.

It was in 1937, the year her book won the Pulitzer, that Old Timer came into Mitchell's life. She had never been able to turn away any stray cat wanting food and always kept an eye on neighbourhood felines and their welfare. Old Timer was an especially disreputable cat, but he found a welcome at the Marsh home (by this time they had moved out of 'the Dump' and were living in the Russell Apartments on Atlanta's Seventeenth Street, very near her parents' old home on Peachtree Street). Mitchell described the feline arrival in a letter as 'a tramp and dirty as a stoker'. He was 'a fine, old, striped animal, a great ladies' man, who has been dropping in for a dish of milk every other night'.[3] Neighbourhood children had teased the cat and she felt sorry for him.

She was even more sympathetic after Old Timer was involved in a bad fight:

> A couple of weeks ago he came calling with all his rear end chewed and mangled and as fine an infection in his equipment as you ever laid eyes on. I put him in the cat hospital and the veterinarians and I labored vainly to save the

> above mentioned equipment. We saved Old Timer, but, alas, the equipment is gone with the wind. He is at home now being fed on yeast and cod liver oil, for I cannot turn a sick animal out. I fear I will never be able to turn him out for he adores the silk brocade of my rocking chair as it makes such a delightful sound when his claws rip into it. Adopting a cat is a serious matter and apt to change one's life as it means becoming a slave to the creature's insistent desires to get out when he's in and in when he's out. But John and I are rapidly succumbing to his charms. He has the most beautiful stand of whiskers you ever saw.[4]

Mitchell delighted in writing to her friend Mabel Granberry about Old Timer.

> Poor Old Timer, who has spent his days in coal cellars and garbage cans, had never heard of catnip and he practically lost his mind. I never saw such antics in all my life, and we finally had to put the catnip mice away for fear that in his weakened condition he would have apoplexy.[5]

Mabel also received regular health updates with possibly more physical detail than she really wanted to hear:

> He is doing very nicely but there is still some infection in his twickey. If I put ointment on the twickey, he licks it off, or else wipes it off on the brocade chair. John has refused to let me put a diaper on him. John says it is shocking enough for a male creature to be bereft of his dearest possessions without having to suffer the final ignominy of a diaper.[6]

Even without an undignified diaper, Old Timer recovered and settled happily into life with the Marshes in Russell Apartments.

Old Timer was not a part of Mitchell's life as she wrote *Gone with the Wind*, but he certainly was in the exciting build-up to the movie. The famous film version premiered in Atlanta in 1939, won ten Academy Awards and was at that point the highest-earning film. The publicity was enormous, but Mitchell preferred spending time with her cat rather than with the movie's stars, and she did her best to avoid media and fans. Old Timer shredded her chairs, deigned to let her open doors for him, graciously accepted the food she gave him, and shared with this famous author the best ten years of his life. Margaret Mitchell never ceased to lament the loss of her cat's 'equipment' – with her strong interest in dirty stories and erotic books (which she collected and shared with friends), she probably felt no respectable male could live a proper life without those necessary parts. But Old Timer seemed to cope and knew he'd found for himself a good and loving home. He moved with them in 1939 when they took up residence in the Della-Manta Apartments in Piedmont Avenue. When he simply vanished in 1947, Mitchell never learned his fate and she missed him greatly.

Old Timer's successor was Count Dracula, a kitten who was so named because he seemed almost to fly through the air and climb vertical surfaces. Mitchell was convinced her kitten's father must have been a flying squirrel. John Marsh had recently suffered a serious heart attack, but remained more tolerant of the kitten's behaviour than was his wife. Count Dracula ran up chairs, attacked pot plants and scattered the soil. He slept all day, and therefore wanted to play at night; 'All that interests him is a romp, a fight, things to eat and not being bothered when he is asleep',[7] Mitchell complained. He proved too much for them and so Count Dracula was given away to owners less in need of rest.

He was followed by Maud, given to the Marshes by a neighbour, Mrs West. Maud was a calico kitten who had been rescued from a sewer. John and Peggy adored her and she slept on John's bed at night. When his mother sent them a gift of a potted African violet, Maud delighted in biting bits off it. She also watched with interest all the birds that came to feed in the bird feeder outside the window. Mitchell fed the birds raisins. Maud, though, would have liked to personally dine on the jays and mockingbirds that fed there. In 1947 Mitchell and Maud featured on the cover of *Sunday Magazine*, along with a history of the creature's name. She was named after a prostitute: John had once heard of a woman of the streets named Maud and thought it an odd name for a woman in that profession – the idea tickled him, and he bestowed it on their cat. The magazine editors, however, thought it would be far more becoming if Mitchell were to say that Tennyson's poem *Maud* was the inspiration – a more decorous and literary choice for a woman who had written a bestseller.

Margaret Mitchell did extensive research for the writing of *Gone with the Wind*. She'd have noted with approval that General Robert E. Lee loved cats. He had Baxter, whose colour he beautifully described as 'moonlight on the water',[8] yellow Tom Tita, and then Tom the Nipper, an excellent mouser. As a Southerner, she naturally detested the very name Abraham Lincoln; but could her hatred have been softened by the knowledge that Lincoln adored cats? When asked if her husband had a hobby, Mary Todd Lincoln replied succinctly that it was cats. When Lincoln found three stray kittens in a telegraph hut in Virginia in 1865, he refused to leave until he'd found good homes for them all.

The soldiers of the Civil War were not supposed to keep pets, but many disobeyed orders. Cats on naval vessels hunted mice and were often embraced as ship mascots. For many soldiers, cats were familiar companions from the homes and farms for which they yearned. Cats raised soldier morale, alleviated boredom and gave comfort to young men facing danger, hunger, cold and an uncertain future. Cats make appearances in grainy Civil War photographs, are mentioned in old letters, and clearly had a part to play in the terrible conflict that tore America apart.

Although felines play no part *in Gone with the Wind*, the real 'cat' of this great Civil War novel is Scarlett O'Hara herself. We first meet her when she's only sixteen: spoiled, learning her power over men, vain and pampered. The first line of the novel tells us that Scarlett is 'not beautiful',[9] but her eyes, those of a 'prowling, hungry cat',[10] are gorgeous and she knows how to use them effectively. Her glamour and seductive charm are very feline qualities, but one knows with Scarlett that the claws are liable to be unsheathed at any moment. Scarlett's story is one of survival, her strong instinct for self-preservation being also cat-like. She is territorial, like a cat, clinging to her beloved home and ruthless in saving it from Yankee soldiers and carpetbaggers. When Scarlett is pleased with life, one can almost hear her purring; when she is unhappy, the hissing and scratching begin. Cats are essentially selfish creatures; Scarlett has that characteristic too.

All three of Scarlett's husbands recognize her feline qualities. Timid, blushing Charles Hamilton is not allowed near Scarlett's bed on their wedding night and is forced to remain uncomfortably in an armchair. When seducing bland and incompetent Frank Kennedy because she wants his money, Scarlett is exactly like a cat – one can imagine her rubbing against his legs and purring. Once unhappily married to him, Scarlett shows 'the temper ... and the rages of a wild cat'[11] and Frank cowers in fear of her. Scarlett, like a cat, despises those who kowtow and make themselves her slaves. Third husband Rhett Butler says to her: 'God help the man who ever really loves you. You'd break his heart, my darling, cruel destructive little cat who is so careless and confident she doesn't even trouble to sheathe her claws.'[12] Scarlett O'Hara is deeply self-absorbed and rarely stops to consider the feelings of others. She knows how to seek out comfort, just like a cat finding its patch of sunlight or soft cushion. And somehow, when she falls, she always seems to land on her feet. She's like a lioness defending Tara from anyone who might snatch her beloved home from her grasp.

Readers of *Gone with the Wind* are gripped as Scarlett lives out some of her nine lives. Then, at the end of the novel, like Old Timer himself, she disappears. Margaret Mitchell was asked endless times about her heroine's fate – did she get Rhett back? Did she end up with Ashley even though she'd realized she had never really loved him? Or did she live out a solitary life at Tara, coming to a recognition of her many faults? Cats are mysterious creatures and like to retain their air of secrecy. Scarlett O'Hara keeps her feline-like mystery at the end of this epic story; we, as readers, will never know what her cats' eyes will see after the tale comes to a close.

It's a nice thought that Vivien Leigh, who so memorably acted Scarlett in the film of *Gone with the Wind*, was also crazy about cats. Her breed of choice was the Siamese. 'Once you have kept a Siamese cat, you would never have any other kind',[13] she insisted. Her first Siamese was given to her by husband Laurence Olivier, and was named New Boy after London's New Theatre. Vivien Leigh considered him her lucky charm and took him everywhere, including to Australia where he was sadly run over. He was followed by Armando. One of her favourites was Poo Jones, a smoky white Siamese, who would fall asleep on her shoulder. He was by Vivien Leigh's side through the health crises of her last years, and with her when she died. Poo Jones was then given a home by Leigh's housekeeper. Margaret Mitchell met Vivien Leigh at the time of the movie premiere. It's to be hoped that the women discussed their mutual love of cats.

On 11 August 1949 Margaret Mitchell was struck by a speeding car on Peachtree Street. She died five days later, without having regained consciousness. She was buried in Atlanta's Oakland Cemetery. John Marsh, who died in 1952, was buried beside his wife. The very last photograph taken of Peggy Mitchell, like the first, shows her holding a cat. Taken just weeks before she died, it is the last piece of evidence of the love of cats which had sustained her throughout life. Shy, red-headed, feisty and tiny (she was 4 feet, 11 inches in low heels), Margaret Mitchell shared many qualities with the animals she loved, and welcomed them with enthusiasm into her tragically brief life.

PAWS FOR THOUGHT
## Theatre cats

Cats who know their 'star' status in the animal kingdom sometimes enjoy treading the boards. Since Elizabethan times they have earned their keep in theatres by controlling rodents feasting on dropped hazelnuts or, perhaps, popcorn.

London's theatres have a rich history of cat-owning. When Joseph Cave took over the Old Vic in 1867, it was rat-infested. His brindled stray killed them, but also reproduced – soon there were twenty cats in residence. Jack and Cleo, Globe Theatre cats in the 1990s, rejoiced in the stage names Brutus and Portia. The Prince of Wales Theatre's cats were, appropriately, William and Harry. If a vet's care was needed, they were taken to one in Harley Street, such was their 'royal' prestige.

Wannabe feline stars have often upstaged actors or distracted audiences. The Albert Theatre's Boy Cat ate Princess Margaret's bouquet at a gala performance, and strutted across the stage during *Pygmalion*. At the Gielgud Theatre 'principal mouser' Beerbohm decided the sand placed on stage for a 1970s' production of *The House of Bernarda Alba* was for use as a handy litter tray, to much audience amusement. Sadler, the cat of Sadler's Wells, was to star in the comic opera *The School for Fathers*, but got stage fright and vamoosed. A January 1956 advertisement called for a replacement: 'WANTED. CAT FOR OPERA APPEARANCES',[14] stating the applicant must be fully grown, accustomed to applause, and possess poise and dignity. Remuneration offered was one sardine and two complimentary tickets per performance. Application had to be in writing – not easy for creatures whose many talents fail to include penmanship.

During the twentieth century most theatres in London and Broadway had resident felines, but health and safety standards, and improved pest control, have reduced their numbers today. The superstitious believed cats brought luck to any theatre. Perhaps it is a purr-fect custom that should be revived?

# BLITZ
## who murdered mice for Dorothy L. Sayers

*Blitz condescended to live with Dorothy L. Sayers, born in Oxford in 1893, died in Witham in 1957, mystery novelist and creator of Lord Peter Wimsey, translator of Dante, and playwright.*

When mystery writer, playwright, poet and religious writer Dorothy L. Sayers died, the very last living creature her eyes beheld was a cat (there were currently three sharing her home). It was 17 December 1957, and she'd returned to her Essex home after Christmas shopping in London. She alighted from the train at Witham and was met there by her usual taxi driver, Jack Lapwood. Sayers was feeling extremely tired and wanted nothing but bath and bed, but first she had to feed her cats, who reminded her noisily that dinner was way beyond its usual time. She walked towards her kitchen. At the foot of the stairs she suffered a stroke and dropped dead. The animals had to wait until the gardener, Mr Bradford, arrived next morning to make the grim discovery and feed the distressed animals. It was a death that, ironically, Sayers had predicted in her writings when her alter ego, fictional Harriet Vane, imagines her own demise: 'Well, one day the usual thing happens. Blinds left down, no smoke from kitchen chimney, milk not taken in, cats yowling fit to break your heart.'[1]

The life that ended so suddenly in Essex had started in Oxford and much of it was cat-less. Even when the Sayers family moved to a Huntingdonshire rectory, her parents felt no need to give their only child a pet. She had imaginary friends in the books she devoured, and if she craved animal company then there was the pony, Jenny, who pulled the trap when the family travelled to town. Once her formal education started, pets for Sayers became an impossibility. Boarding school in Salisbury was no place for pets, and nor was Somerville College, Oxford (Sayers was one of the very first Oxford women to graduate), although possibly there was a college cat. She then went teaching in Hull, worked for some time at Blackwell's Bookshop in Oxford, and briefly lived in France. Her unsettled lifestyle and penury made it hard to care for a cat. It was only in the 1920s, when Sayers moved to London and found steady employment, that a cat was first thought of. And it was mice that can be held responsible.

At the end of 1920 she took a three-year lease on a small flat in Great James Street, Bloomsbury. She loved her three rooms and new independence, but the place was plagued by rodents. Mice rampaged through the flat, nibbled at her scant food supplies and frightened her at night. In June 1922 she wrote to her mother to explain her solution to the problem:

> I have got a lodger! – the mice were getting so bad in my kitchen that I asked my char to find me a kitten, and she has just produced one. It arrived today – a vulgar little tabby Tom, but very quick and lively. I should think he would be a very good mouser ... I shall either call him Peter (after Lord Peter), or Agag, because he walks delicately.[2]

Agag was what he became. Sayers, daughter of an Anglican rector, knew her Bible. Her choice of name referenced the book of Samuel: 'Then said Samuel, Bring ye hither to me Agag the king of the Amalekites. And Agag came unto him delicately.'[3]

The diet of mice suited Agag to perfection and he was soon a monstrous size. Sayers liked to lie with her head pillowed on works of criminology, cigarette in mouth and Agag comfortably settled on her tummy – it was exactly what she needed for contemplating the next twist in her detective plots. He featured in her letters home and in December 1928 was sending his love in letters to her mother.

Agag soon had companions, for in 1926 Dorothy married 'Mac' Fleming, and in 1927 another cat, Adelbert joined the establishment. Perhaps Agag had grown too fat and lazy to hunt efficiently, for the mice were again a problem: 'On account of the extreme voracity, agility and fecundity of the mice, we have had to get a new kitten. It is very small and hasn't caught any mice as yet, but no doubt it will before long.'[4] The charlady overfed Adelbert, who then had to be dosed with castor oil.

Adelbert caused quite a shock when he went missing in April. One evening Mac came hurriedly to his wife, asking 'Where's the kitten?' Together they searched the flat, calling for Adelbert. Thinking he must have somehow slipped out, they searched stairs, backyard and even other flats in the building. No kitten. But Dorothy wasn't giving up: she 'sought him at the greengrocer's, the milk-shop, the pub and in all the surrounding streets'. Sadly, they had to resign themselves to the loss of their pet. Sayers, a religious woman, sent up prayers and promised St Anthony a candle if he would only restore Adelbert to them. She'd hardly finished praying when Mac rushed in with the news that the kitten had been found. That morning, when the bed was made, the cat had been made up with it – 'right under a heavy hair mattress, between that and the box-spring bed with the blankets tucked tightly in all round ... He had been made up in the bed for 10 hours in a state – one would suppose – of complete suffocation! He seemed none the worse, except that he was very hungry.' The promised candle wasn't forgotten, 'for S. Anthony is a keen man of business and does not care to be trifled with.'[5] Sayers later used Adelbert's misadventure in a short story, broadcast over the radio in 1954, in which Lord Peter Wimsey tells of how, as a boy, he lost his kitten and Sherlock Holmes had to be called in. The great detective suggested that the boy look under his mattress.

In 1928 Sayers decided they needed bigger rooms and she, Mac, Adelbert and Agag were able to rent a larger flat upstairs in the same building. Before moving in, however, new carpets were laid. Agag loved the excitement: 'the cat is investigating the mysterious cavities between the joists of the flooring, with a view to getting nailed down under the floor, if possible',[6] she reported. Both cats loved going up on the roof – a grimy and smoky place, in Dorothy's opinion, but cats adore vantage points. Adelbert was a clever animal 'who will run after balls of paper and bring them back to you to throw, just like a dog',[7] but he was too prone to enter into fights with other Bloomsbury felines.

In October of that year Dorothy and Mac purchased a country house in Witham, Essex. From there she travelled to and from London, seeing publishers and supervising the productions of the plays she wrote. Fortunately, Mac loved the cats and was happy to stay home with them. She was the breadwinner, while Mac was the domestic partner who tended the animals.

In 1932 a cat she finally named Peter, after her fictional creation, joined their home. It turned out he should have been named Petra instead, for Peter produced four kittens. Two had to be drowned and Dorothy sketched them rising from the bucket and ascending to 'other spheres'. One kitten, named Squeaker ('because he squeaks if you pick him up'), was found a home elsewhere. The remaining one was kept and called Thomas Yownie after the boy in John Buchan's 1922 novel *Huntingtower* 'because nothing ever upsets him'. Buchan was Scottish so Thomas was soon answering to 'Tammas' (a cat named Tammas Yownie is briefly mentioned in Sayers's great novel *Gaudy Night*). In colouring he 'had a grey striped back and a white front underneath a white face ... He is very ugly, but very intelligent.'[8] In 1933 Peter had another litter – one kitten was given to the local butcher. Peter's owners hoped that his fecundity would be 'moderate' in the future.[9]

Some time in the 1930s a cat named Wilkie was added to the Witham menagerie. He was named for groundbreaking detective novelist Wilkie Collins. Like his namesake, though, Wilkie suffered from ill health: 'he was a little potty. He died, deeply regretted, of some trouble in his throat.'[10]

During World War II Sayers took in cats belonging to friends who were worried about pet safety during the Blitz. Like Dr Johnson, she shopped personally for their food as she didn't want to submit her servant to this indignity. Feeding the animals wasn't easy with rationing in full force, so perhaps more mice were caught during these lean years? Poultry attract rodents, of course, and Sayers kept chickens, keeping up a habit of bestowing literary names on them: Elinor and Marianne were named for the heroines of Jane Austen's *Sense and Sensibility*; the staid and sensible bird was Elinor, while Marianne was scatty and heedless. Elinor died a few months later; then Jane and Elizabeth, two pullets, arrived in the poultry yard, causing Marianne to create a 'shocking fuss'[11] from jealousy. Friend and fellow writer C.S. Lewis was always much interested in these Austenian birds' antics. There was also a pig, delightfully named Francis Bacon (after the Elizabethan writer and statesman). But Sayers was never sentimental about the animals – Francis Bacon and his successor Fatima ended their lives ingloriously on her dinner plate, as did the chickens.

It was difficult feeding pets in wartime, for ration books covered people, not pets. Sayers hated seeing her cats go hungry, and she wrote a poem addressed to one of them, showing her regret over its meagre meals. 'War Cat' begins with an apology:

> I am sorry, my little cat, I am sorry –
> If I had it, you should have it;
> But there is a war on.
> No, there are no table-scraps;
> there was only an omelette
> made from dehydrated eggs,
> and baked apples to follow,
> and we finished it all.
> The butcher has no lights,
> the fishmonger has no cod's heads –

there is nothing for you
but cat-biscuit
and those remnants of yesterday's ham;
you must do your best with it...[12]

In the second half of the poem, we get the voice of the cat. Why, it asks plaintively, when it has killed mice and even stoats as part of its personal war effort, has rubbed itself against her legs to show devotion and tried hard to eat the unappetizing contents of the cat bowl, does she not reward him with something edible? Finally, Sayers tips the contents of the bowl into the chicken scraps dish and dons coat and hat to set off to the butcher's when, suddenly, the cat decides it can eat the food after all and tucks into the bowl intended for the poultry. The poem ends with the poet feeling that, although her cat has made a fool of her, she will visit the butcher anyway and see what morsels can be purchased. It's a delightful and humorous verse, showing how Sayers, who relished good food, shared her cat's outrage at the lack of decent meat.

In the war, like so many women, she knitted. To ease the boredom of the task, she invented a pattern inspired by the coat of a tabby cat (probably Agag, who'd have been around fourteen by this time). The character Miss Milsom does the same in her novel *The Documents in the Case*.

Early in the war, Sayers made an excursion to London. Walking along a street that had suffered bomb damage, she came across a sight guaranteed to pull at her heartstrings – a tiny ginger kitten sheltering in the rubble. She took him home with her that day and named him Blitz.[13] Perhaps killing the mice in the kitchen failed to appeal to Blitz, for Sayers regularly queued at Holt's the fishmonger and butcher of Witham (the shop, which opened in the High Street in 1953, still operates as a butcher and delicatessen today) to buy him fish. Soon Blitz was appearing in her correspondence and promised to 'dedicate his next mouse'[14] to her friend Charis Barnett. Knowing how important he was to her, her friends rarely forgot to send Blitz personal festive greetings. His doings regularly appeared in her correspondence. 'Blitz is very well, and having a great time with "joy and giblets", as we had partridges for dinner yesterday',[15] she reported to close friend Norah Lambourne. In 1947 she wrote to Norah to let her know that Blitz's brief loss of appetite had suddenly been cured: 'I fear his malady was sheer naughty jealousy and sulks.'[16] To stimulate the lost appetite the cat was given 'three cat powders'.[17] In 1953 he had teeth problems which proved costly: 'Poor old Blitz has been having a bad time. He came out with a beastly sort of abscess, discharging through one of his tear-ducts, and had a dreadful eye.'[18] Mr Walker, the local vet, 'scraped all his teeth and then put him under an anaesthetic and yanked out a decayed molar. The old man took everything very stoically and earned great admiration.'[19]

Blitz has been wonderfully commemorated by his inclusion in the statue of Sayers which stands in the street outside her Witham home. It was designed by sculptor John Doubleday, whose idea it was to include the cat. He remembered, when young, seeing Sayers out shopping for Blitz's meals – 'she was an unusual sight', he recalled, 'wearing a fur coat, which was far from new, contrasting with plimsolls by way of footwear.'[20] His original plan was to have the cat brushing past her leg on approaching her, but the committee commissioning the statue felt it would be inappropriate to have the animal's bottom facing outwards and requested that Blitz be turned around. John Doubleday also wanted to portray the author in her furs, but again the committee protested, insisting the furs be removed as a concession to animal rights enthusiasts, even though it was virtually her uniform when on any outing. The statue was, appropriately, unveiled by crime writer P.D. James in August 2000 (P.D. James shared her home with a succession of Burmese cats). Bronzed Blitz, tail in air, stands at his mistress's feet, as if asking for more fishy delicacies to be placed in his dinner bowl. He has been very popular with passing children, who stop to stroke him. As a result, his back is shinier than the rest of him.

Several of Dorothy's friends shared her love of cats, and her letters contain feline greetings for her correspondents. Sharing their sorrow, she wrote poems when friends' cats died. Her Oxford friends Muriel St Clare Byrne and her partner Marjorie Barber (called Bar by DLS) together wrote a book of advice for cat-lovers in 1925, with notes about vet care and lists of chemists who sold feline medicines. The book supplies a recipe for 'stomach trouble' – egg white, brandy, sugar and water – to be administered every three hours. Not perhaps something a vet would recommend today. Bar wrote a story in which a cat named Mr Darcy puts in an appearance. When Bar and Muriel's white Persian, Timothy, died in 1928, Sayers wrote the poem 'For Timothy, in the Coinherence' (the coinherence is the innate relationship of all life to God) in which she insisted that it is easier to live up to one's moral standards with cats than with people. Another Oxford friend, Dorothy Rowe, penned 'Epitaph on a Cat'.

Her friend Norah Lambourne also loved cats. In the war Norah often came to stay, bringing Bramble in a basket, and sometimes the cat spent weeks with Dorothy when Norah had to travel for work (she was an artist and theatre designer). The two women together created *A Cat's Christmas Carol*, an eight-page pamphlet with six linocuts by Norah and a poem by Dorothy. This was posted out to ailurophile friends (T.S. Eliot was one recipient). When Bramble was at Witham, he was included in the seasonal greetings sent from her cats, 'Bramble, Sandra, George and Tibby Tandrum'.[21] After the war Sayers translated Tasso's sonnet from Italian into English as 'Torquato Tasso to the Cats of St Anne's,' and gave the translation to cat-loving friends as part of her Christmas card.[22]

Dorothy Sayers's marriage to Mac was a troubled one, due mainly to his drinking, and she considered ending it at one time. But they did share a love of cats and he was always there to feed them when she was away, although by 1948 Blitz was an 'only cat'. Mac died in 1950. That same year Dorothy acquired a new tabby, named George Macaulay Trevelyan (usually just George), after the historian who had nominated D.L. Sayers that year for an honorary degree at Durham University. Blitz was at first hostile, but soon the cats were romping happily together. George was clearly the dominant animal and stole Blitz's food: 'Blitz is too gentlemanly (or too thick-headed) to cuff his ears for him, and when his plate is invaded just turns away with a resigned and melancholy look and has to be rescued.'[23] Six months after Mac's death, she took George with her when she went to stay with Muriel and Bar for Christmas. With a bag of books under one arm, and George under the other, Dorothy saw herself as the perfect travelling spinster. Her thank-you letter was penned by

George to 'Auntie Mew and Auntie Purr' and wished both ladies a 'purrspurous New Year'.[24]

Dorothy L. Sayers grew more reclusive in her later years, rarely travelling to London and working quietly on her translation of Dante, but Blitz and George were wonderful company and she loved them dearly. The cats even had the huge privilege of hearing her recite Dante to them and liked to lie on her substantial bosom 'kneading dough',[25] or bite the pen and tread on the pages as she wrote.

In 1952 John, the illegitimate son she never publicly acknowledged, acquired a cat, who was named Gilbert. George and Blitz (sometimes referred to as 'the Pussies',[26] always with a capital *P*) frequently sent Gilbert their love. 'A good cat', she told John, 'matures richly like a full-bodied wine and is at his best, I think, after about seven years in bottle and three in the wood.'[27] She herself had 'four mewing mouths to be filled with fish four times in every day', she complained,[28] but she simply could not resist more cats or turn away a hungry stray.

In 1953 Sandra joined the household: 'a stray female of unknown origin ... relentlessly adopted us, and apparently proposes to burden us with an unspecified number of totally unwanted kittens', she complained.[29] Four kittens duly arrived – highly inconvenient, as she was undergoing house renovations at the time. But Sandra was soon a fixture. So, on some nights, was Sandra's boyfriend, a 'repulsive' neighbouring cat who sneaked in, peed, romped with Sandra and departed, leaving her expecting yet again.[30] Strangely, Sayers never seems to have considered taking Sandra to the helpful Mr Walker to have her spayed (the spaying and neutering of cats and dogs had become accessible and widely available by the 1930s). The last years of Sayers's life were made anxious by the fate of various litters and finding 'eligible situations for young cats'.[31] Kittens 'dance on my chest at night', she told her friend and future biographer, Barbara Reynolds,[32] while their mother, trying to teach her offspring how to hunt, brought dead sparrows to the bedroom, or left headless mice under chests of drawers. One kitten went in 1955 to writer and broadcaster Val Gielgud; another went to Le Moulin d'Or, a French restaurant in London in need of a skilled mouser (Sayers often recommended the restaurant to friends, telling them to look out for the cat when there). Sandra presented her with litters in 1954, 1955, 1956 and 1957. It all made her feel that she was running a cat factory and should hang out a sign:

CAT'S PARADISE
Board residence
On and Off Milk Licence
(Non-Residents Served)
Maison Tolérée
Proprietress: D.L. Sayers.[33]

She called her feline production business 'Kittens Unlimited', and advertised each 'fresh assignment' as

'House-trained, Mouse-trained',[34] but because she had high standards for their future homes it could be hard to place Sandra's offspring. Her friend the Reverend Moody took a black kitten, but perhaps Sayers's boast was inaccurate, because he was soon writing to complain about nasty deposits left on his bed by the new arrival.

In January 1957 she gave food and shelter to a stray tom, whom she named Poor Papa. When she found him badly injured, Mr Walker was again called on to help. Poor Papa was given penicillin and his torn legs sewn up. Briefly she thought of renaming him Marsyas, after the satyr of Greek myth who dared to challenge Apollo to a musical contest and was flayed alive for his presumption, but the old name stuck, and Poor Papa continued to drop in every so often for meals. When she had heaters installed in the library all her cats were delighted and curled up as close to the new equipment as they could get.

With so many felines in her life, it is hardly surprising that Dorothy L. Sayers should have included cats in her fiction. In the last of the Lord Peter books, *Busman's Honeymoon*, Harriet admires her new husband relaxing in a window seat with a ginger cat on his lap – 'two sleek animals together',[35] she notes. Lord Peter is the younger son of the aristocratic Denver family, whose coat of arms features a domestic cat 'couched as to spring'.[36] Cats are not uncommon in heraldry, though wildcats are more usual than domestic cats (a wildcat's ferocity was prized by ancient dynasties).[37] Lord Peter finds a discarded cat brooch near a corpse in *Clouds of Witness* and has to sleuth until he learns who dropped it there. Peter's mother, the lovable Dowager Duchess of Denver, has a cat named Ahasuerus (the name of several Hebrew rulers in the Bible), who naughtily leaves a mouse in her maid Franklin's shoe. When Lord Peter establishes an employment bureau to help struggling spinsters, he calls it The Cattery. *Murder Must Advertise* depicts journalist Hector Puncheon 'interviewing' a cat who has raised the alarm over a warehouse fire. He goes on to secure good homes for the said cat's offspring.

Sayers makes use of ailurophobia (a terror of cats) in the plots of two of her stories. In 1933 she published a Montague Egg tale (he is her other fictional detective) entitled 'Maher-Shalal-Hashbaz' in which a rich, elderly, ailurophobic man with heart disease is deliberately frightened to death. His family, who want his money, smuggle fifty cats into his room while he is sleeping. In the 1939 short story 'The Cyprian Cat' the narrator suffers from such severe ailurophobia that he can sense a cat's presence without setting eyes on it. This fear leads him to shoot at a cat he is convinced is haunting him, but what he shoots is his friend's oddly cat-like wife, and he is arrested for murder. The story of 'The Fantastic Horror of the Cat in the Bag' sadly fails to include any felines, but simply makes general use of the known mysteriousness of cats. In her

Miltonic parody *Pussydise Lost* Sayers imagines pet owners as gods, and depicts the bewilderment of the cat praised for killing a rodent and rebuked for killing a songbird:

> Why are the trees of Paradise
> Set round with prohibitions?
> The gods, mysterious and all-wise,
> Impose these strange conditions.[38]

By the end of 1952 Blitz was getting very old and feeble and Sayers worried about this favourite of all her felines. But with her kind care and solicitate, and plenty of fish, Blitz lived on. Sayers was convinced that he regretted never having visited the Norwegian town of Bergen 'with all that lovely fish about',[39] but Blitz snoozed contentedly in her armchair. In January 1954 she wrote to her son: 'My beloved and aged Blitz is now nearly fifteen, and getting very rickety on his legs, poor old man, but he is the wisest and best of the lot, and as long as he can enjoy his sleep and food and a seat by the fire, I propose to look after him.'[40] She can't ever have been sure of his exact birthday, but could guess his age from his size when she first found him. Blitz did make it to fifteen and died that year, cherished and loved to the last. It was a lucky day for one small ginger kitten when a mystery novelist who loved cats found him on a bomb site.

## PAWS FOR THOUGHT
# T.S. Eliot's cat poems

In 1939 future Nobel Prize-winning poet[41] T.S. Eliot, author of 'The Hollow Men', *The Waste Land* and *Four Quartets*, brought out a very different sort of poetry book which reflected his personal passion for cats (it was a family trait – his businessman father had loved to doodle cats on commercial documents). *Old Possum's Book of Practical Cats* was the result of letters and poems written for his godchildren. It was published by Faber & Faber, the company for which he worked. The cover was illustrated by the author.

This delightful volume contains some classic poems about the psychology, sociology and behaviour of cats, with Eliot drawing on his long experience of living with felines (his cats included Jellylorum, Pettipaws (who was pernickety about food and only wanted to eat rabbit), Wiscus, Zuaxo and George Pushdragon. The volume, which opens with 'The Naming of Cats', includes 'Macavity: The Mystery Cat', 'Gus: The Theatre Cat', 'Skimbleshanks: The Railway Cat', 'Growltiger's Last Stand', 'Old Deuteronomy' and 'Mungojerrie and Rumpelteazer'. The poems are whimsical and funny – one feels that Eliot let his hair down (so to speak) in the writing of them. The book sold far better than did any of his other volumes of poetry and has been translated into many languages.

He is the 'Old Possum' of the title (it was a name Ezra Pound bestowed on him). He had clearly enjoyed reciting cat poems to his godchildren, and including them in the letters he wrote them, so fortunately he decided to share his poems with the world. The verses illustrate his view that cats possess two qualities to an extreme degree – dignity and comicality. Those are exactly the qualities his cat poems possess. His second wife, Valerie, who preferred dogs, stated that cats had a special place in his affection. Eliot once spent a delightful evening with Groucho Marx, discussing good cigars and cats.

*Old Possum's Book of Practical Cats* was the inspiration for the hugely popular Andrew Lloyd Webber musical *Cats*. It premiered in London in 1981 and on Broadway in 1982, and became the longest-running Broadway show in history (until another Andrew Lloyd Webber production overtook it).

> Again I must remind you that
> A Dog's a Dog – A CAT'S A CAT.[42]

# SAMBO
## who helped Paul Gallico remain in a state of delusion

*Sambo condescended to live with Paul Gallico, born in New York in 1897, died in Monaco or Antibes, France, in 1976, journalist, sportswriter and novelist.*

From boyhood Paul Gallico longed for a cat. If only he could have a kitten! Oh, how he yearned for a small furry bundle to love! He wasn't fussy as to breed – Siamese, Persian, Manx or plain tabby – any sort would be just fine. He'd accept any colour, whether black or white, grey or brown, or a mixture of them all, although, if pressed, he'd admit to a sneaking fondness for ginger cats. Again and again he begged his parents – please, please could he have a cat?

This was the constant refrain of Paul Gallico's childhood, and it's a longing he gave his boy hero, the lonely Peter, in *Jennie*, the moving novel he wrote about a cat. But Gallico grew up in a New York apartment, the son of an Italian pianist and composer and an Austrian mother, and his parents were too busy making progress as new American migrants to spend time or money on a pet for their often neglected son. Like young Peter, Paul had to make do with chance encounters, fussing over cats he met in the park or the street.

As a young man, Paul Gallico could offer no settled home to a cat. He studied science at Columbia University. In World War I he served in the US army, worked briefly as a movie reviewer, and then began his distinguished career in sports journalism, kick-started when he invited boxer Jack Dempsey to box with him. The resulting article vividly described what it felt like to be knocked unconscious by a professional only two minutes into the first round. Gallico's journalism took him everywhere – playing golf with Bobby Jones, catching a baseball thrown by Dizzy Dean, founding the Golden Gloves amateur boxing competition. His sports reports hit just the right note with Americans; he is today regarded as one of the first celebrity sports writers. His first major book was *Farewell to Sport*. But Gallico, just as he had always longed to be owned by a cat, had also always wanted to write fiction. Sport was a well-paying but temporary job for him. In 1936 he sold a short story to the movies for $5,000, which enabled him to retire from journalism permanently.

This was not the only change in his life. That same year, having divorced his second wife Elaine, he moved to England. There he purchased a house in Salcombe, South Devon, and began writing fiction. More than forty books followed, including *The Adventures of Hiram Holiday* (1939), *The Snow Goose* (1941), *Mrs. 'Arris Goes to Paris* (1958) and its three delightful sequels, *Manxmouse* (1968) – a book J.K. Rowling adored – and *The Poseidon Adventure* (1969), which became one of the first disaster movies and has remained a cult classic. Paul Gallico made an excellent income from writing and film rights. He once confessed that he was 'a rotten novelist',[1] but his fans didn't agree. Several of his works were bestsellers.

Once established in his English house on the hill (called Landmark, it has fabulous sea views), away from an unhappy wife (and not yet married to wife number three, Pauline), Gallico was finally able to realize his childhood ambition. The man who was convinced that he, many generations before, had indeed been a cat, was going to have himself a cat – and not just one cat, but lots of them. He collected strays; those cats had kittens; friends gave him cats; and before he knew it he was sharing his home with twenty-three cats. Their 'protector' was a Great Dane, but surely the cats were in charge and the dog understood his lowly place in the pecking order? Gallico smoked his pipe, strolled in the garden dictating his novels to personal assistant Merrilyn (who today publishes books as Mel Menzies) and enjoyed the company of his cats. He was never fussy as to number or breed – his cats came in all shades and sizes – and he loved to ponder the essential mystery of their natures. Why, he wondered, does a cat purr? 'No one has been able to figure out how they make that subtle sound, and furthermore, no one ever will. It is a secret that has endured since the beginning of cat times and will never be revealed.'[2] Cats and kittens played on his desk, climbed curtains, interfered with his typing and, by their presence, satisfied 'all the pent-up childhood longings'[3] for feline companionship. For Gallico, everything about cats was stimulating, precious and charming.

Although enslaved to so many cats, Paul Gallico never lost the restless streak of his youth, and for the rest of his life he moved frequently. He married his third wife, Pauline, in 1939, and together they moved around England. From 1943 to 1946 he was a war correspondent; after the war his research took him to Europe. He moved on to live on a New Jersey farm, in a Mexican hacienda, in a chalet in Liechtenstein, and in a Malibu beach house – all homes he shared with cats. He eventually settled in Monaco. After divorcing Pauline in 1954, he took off on a 10,000-mile car trip around his home country, a trip sponsored by *Reader's Digest* (taking no cats with him). He married Virginia, his fourth and last wife, in 1963 and they settled firstly in Monaco and then, for the last four years of his life, in Antibes in the South of France.

But wherever in the world Paul Gallico made his home, and no matter which wife he shared it with, cats were always a fixture. He grew convinced that authors needed cats – their constant silent observance forced writers to be more self-aware, more likely to analyse themselves and others. Such awareness made for better writing.

With such a deep love of feline companionship, it's hardly surprising that Paul Gallico made cats the subject of several books. *Jennie*, published in 1950 (the US edition was titled *The Abandoned*) has become a modern classic, never out of print. It's the story of lonely Peter, whose parents neglect him and who has been told repeatedly that he cannot have a cat. 'He had wanted a cat ever since he could remember, which was many years ago at the age of four – when he had gone to stay on a farm near Gerrards Cross, and had been taken into the kitchen and shown a basketful of kittens, orange and white balls of fluff, and the ginger-coloured mother who beamed with pride.'[4] Peter lives in London and has made the acquaintance of all the neighbourhood cats. He smuggles strays home, but Nanny turfs them out angrily. One day, out in the square where he lives, he spots a striped kitten; in dashing out to greet it, he is struck by a car and badly injured. Peter wakes in hospital, or at least he thinks he wakes, and suddenly finds himself transformed into a white cat.

Believing him another nasty stray, Nanny throws him out into the street and the world becomes a very frightening place.

For Peter, while he might look like a cat, has no understanding of how to act like one. He's in serious danger, from territorial strays, from cars, and from starvation because he has no idea how to catch a mouse. And it is then that a wonderful heroine appears – Jennie, a thin tabby with grey-green, gold-flecked eyes. Jennie adopts him and teaches him – how to wash ('If in doubt, wash WASH!' is Jennie's mantra), how to kill vermin, how to find shelter. Together they travel to Scotland in the hope that Jennie can locate feline relations there, and their challenges and travels forge a close bond. Gallico captures in this charming novel the very essence of being a cat. His years of closely watching his own cats and kittens gave him the knowledge of feline mannerisms and behaviour which permeates this book.

His next cat book was also partly narrated by a cat. *Thomasina, the Cat who Thought She Was God*, published in 1957, is set in Scotland in 1912. Young Mary Ruadh's ginger puss Thomasina is disliked by her veterinary father. He tries to kill the cat, but Thomasina is left in a coma. When she emerges from this, lessons are learned by many in the community – a redemptive tale. It was made into the Disney film *The Three Lives of Thomasina*, starring Patrick McGoohan, Susan Hampshire and Karen Dotrice.

As Paul Gallico typed his manuscripts, he often had cats playing on his desk, reaching out their paws to 'help' him type. It was this habit that gave him the idea for his next cat book. *The Silent Miaow: A Manual for Kittens, Strays and Homeless Cats* does not credit Gallico as its author. Rather, the title page announces that the book has been 'Translated from the Feline and Edited by Paul Gallico'. Gallico framed the book with an unusual pretence. He claimed that his publisher, finding manuscript pages on his doorstep one morning, struggled to read the peculiar mix of letters. Knowing that Paul Gallico had wartime decoding experience, the publisher showed him the pages. But the problem seemed unsolvable – no known cipher had such a mix of letters and numbers. Then Gallico had a brainwave – such mistakes were exactly what a cat would make when placing its paw on one typewriter key but accidentally hitting letters either side because of the paw's breadth. With that knowledge, Gallico is able to translate this 'astonishing literary find'[5] and publish it.

*The Silent Miaow*'s author is a cat who lost its mother when a kitten. She's had to learn the ways of humans without maternal guidance, and wants to share her hard-won knowledge with other felines. This cat's manual is packed with good advice about manipulating humans – how to insinuate yourself into a good home, which errors to avoid (shedding fur on sofas), how to be accepted on the human's bed, how to play on the insecurities of male owners (bachelors are considered especially desirable as cat owners) and how never to underestimate female owners. There's even a chapter on how to two-time (being fed in two different establishments, without either owner finding out). Every person who has lived with a cat will know the frustration of cats' eating habits. One places before puss a dish she happily ate yesterday, only to have her reject it disdainfully. The book dedicates a chapter to food – how to train your human to offer variety, proffer the right delicacies and win the battle of wills over dinner. This feline advice should result in meals of 'Alaska king crab claws, stewed lightly in Czechoslovakian butter, served on a bed of French anchovy toast'.[6] There are helpful notes on opening doors, enduring travel, the joyful destruction of Christmas decorations, and a chapter on kittens (the female author has had one litter, but found kittens too troublesome to bother having a second).

The book's title comes from 'the silent miaow treatment', something that must be learned by any self-respecting cat wanting to dominate its human. 'You look up at the subject, open your mouth as you would for a fully articulated miaow ... you permit no sound to issue.'[7] This picture of helplessness and misery should invariably prove effective.

Paul Gallico, who wrote the Foreword, admitted that the book is 'a sadly disillusioning revelation'[8] to humans, and accepts that cat owners harbouring deluded feelings of superiority will be shocked to learn how their pets have manipulated them.

The 'manual' came out in 1964. Its 'Afterword' makes a rare reference by name to one of Gallico's own adored cats – Sambo, a smoky grey. He'd been missing for two days and two nights and Gallico went seeking him:

> I encountered him walking up the road from the direction of a neighbourhood where the houses are far larger and wealthier than mine. With my work in translating *The Silent Miaow* fresh in my mind, I was moved to suspicion immediately. Was Sambo two-timing me? In what mansion on the right side of the railroad tracks was he being fed, pampered, and accepted as belonging to them? A momentary pang of fierce jealousy shot through me, to be instantly dispelled. Sambo two-time me? Not *my* cat! I picked him up, chucked him under the chin, and asked him where he'd been. He put his foot in my mouth, rubbed his head against my face, and began to purr violently. There was no point in pursuing the subject further. He was obviously, as always, absolutely mad about me.[9]

And thus Paul Gallico kept his illusions, even after 'translating' a chapter on felines who two-time. Cats, he knew, ensure 'human failing to resist truth and accept only what [one] wishes to believe'.[10]

Paul Gallico's last cat book, *Honorable Cat*, is his least successful. Published in 1972, it's an anthology, a potpourri of literary pieces, dedicated to the world's cats:

Cats of the world arise
This book is dedicated to you all
And your obvious superiority to mankind.
Arise! Unite! Take Over![11]

The book's various essays include one on ailurophobes, those oddities who detest cats. Why does a cat always go to such a person – is it from pity, a perverted sense of humour, or simply the attraction of opposites? Another essay praises feline cleanliness. (Gallico has no time for kitty litter, a product by then widely used in the USA, although less common in the UK.[12]) Others discuss a cat's refusal to be trained (a sign of high intelligence), or describe the mating instinct – his own Siamese, Lulu, when on heat, miaowed ceaselessly and 'struck attitudes on the rug reminiscent of paintings of famous goddesses or courtesans preparing for a night's work'.[13] Lulu had to be let out. The result? Kittens! 'Kittens can happen to anyone',[14] Gallico once admitted cheerfully.

The book also contains poems, including a parody of William Blake's big-cat poem *The Tyger*: 'What immortal hand did make / Me and also William Blake?'[15] its cat narrator asks.

There are poems about feline pastimes – chasing butterflies, finding the most comfortable chair, catching birds, camouflage, and striking graceful attitudes. There's an array of cats' nursery rhymes for mother puss to share with kittens. However, Gallico was not as accomplished a poet as he was a novelist. There's little in this last cat book to be eulogized or remembered. *Honorable Cat* is a compendium of cat lore and cat humour, but the book seems unfocused and lacks the charm of his fiction. Nevertheless, it's a book that speaks volubly of Paul Gallico's own happy thraldom to felines. He'd have thought it entirely appropriate to hand the last word of this chapter over to one of the cats that have their say in his book:

> When I have things to say
> I expect you to listen to me.
> If you cannot understand what I am saying
> That is your fault and your loss,
> But at least be quiet when I am speaking
> And try to comprehend
> You who think yourselves so clever.[16]

## PAWS FOR THOUGHT
## Nursery-rhyme cats

For many, the first encounter with a cat comes through nursery rhymes. In old songs and poems for the very young, cats play many fascinating roles. They might play the fiddle ('Hey Diddle Diddle'), lose their mittens or get them soiled ('The Three Little Kittens') or travel to London in order to meet royalty ('Pussy Cat, Pussy Cat, Where Have You Been?'). There are strange marriages, such as a cat marrying a bumblebee in a version of 'Fiddle-de-Dee! Fiddle-de-Dee!'

Or the cat might look unusual – in 'There Was a Crooked Man' the man owns a 'crooked cat which caught a crooked mouse'.[17] Of course, many nursery rhymes are considered to have hidden meanings and may not be about cats at all, but child readers are unaware of political or sexual undertones and simply enjoy the appearance of a familiar animal in rhymes.

Nursery rhymes also teach children about kindness to felines. In 'Ding Dong Bell' a cat has been dropped into a well by Little Johnny Flynn, but is pulled out by Little Tommy Stout – the young soon recognize which boy is worth emulating. The oldest recorded version of that nursery rhyme (it comes in many variations) dates from 1580, so children have clearly been warned against cruelty to dumb animals for a long time. The rhyme 'I Love Little Pussy', which dates from 1830, encourages gentle patting, never treading on a cat's paw or pulling its tail.

Cats have also been used in teaching juvenile logic. In 'St Ives' a man has seven wives. Each of those wives carries seven sacks, every sack holds seven cats, and every cat has seven kittens. At the end of the rhyme the question is asked, what is the total number travelling to St Ives. Traditionally the correct answer is 'one', as all the others are coming *from* St Ives, but if children do their multiplication correctly there would be 343 cats and 2,401 kittens.

# BLUEBELL
## who critiqued Dame Muriel Spark's manuscripts

*Bluebell condescended to live with Muriel Spark, born in Edinburgh, Scotland, in 1918, died in Florence, Italy, in 2006, novelist, poet, essayist and short-story writer.*

Dame Muriel Spark was rather like a cat herself. Impeccably groomed, secretive and reserved, fiercely independent, and with a tendency to spit when attacked. And yet her early life was spent without cats: her childhood in middle-class Edinburgh, the period of her disastrous marriage in Rhodesia, and her years in London, poverty-stricken as she struggled to make her name as a writer – none of these times was enhanced by felines. Her relationship with her only son, Robin, was deteriorating and would only worsen. There had been a messy love affair with a man who used her, and Muriel was starting to feel that humans were not a very likeable species. So, in 1954, she left London for the Kent countryside, suffering nervous collapse and badly in need of feline comfort. It was there, in a cottage in the grounds of Allington Castle (owned by Carmelite nuns) that she worked on her first novel, *The Comforters*. She had recently converted to Catholicism, a decision which upset many who knew her, and she needed a period of quiet reflection to understand the effect her new religion was having on her and her writing. In the cottage she lived simply on eggs, baked beans and white bread, and relished the peace and the opportunity to focus on her work. Then, unexpectedly, the 'perfect cat'[1] entered her life.

The blue-grey half-Persian kitten was a stray, delivered into Muriel Spark's care by a neighbour, Miss Martin (affectionately called Martie by Muriel). Soon the kitten was a vital and adored companion, completely at home in the cottage. Novelists usually think carefully about names – characters in fiction need exactly the right moniker – and Spark gave serious consideration to the naming of her pet. She chose Bluebell, a name that had strong emotional resonance for her. Bluebell was not named for a flower, but rather for a dress. Her maternal grandmother, Adelaide Uezzell, had once owned a blue silk brocade dress, which she wore to a fancy-dress party, topping it with a hat adorned with fake flowers, and carrying a basket of blooms on her arm. She won a prize for her efforts and loved telling her granddaughter the story of the award-winning outfit. Years later the blue dress was cut up to make cushion covers – Spark later regretted turning its 'deep and heavy brocaded blueness' into such useful items.[2] Perhaps the dress was, as her biographer Martin Stannard suggests, a sort of talisman of the might-have-beens in her intelligent grandmother's life? Perhaps Muriel simply remembered its texture and sensuous beauty with pleasure, so gave the name to her sensuous and elegant cat?

Bluebell was beautiful, although 'her origins were of no particular account'.[3] Perhaps the mixed-breed nature of her cat also appealed to Spark – she herself had always felt 'different', with a Jewish father and a Presbyterian mother, one parent Scottish and the other English.

> [Bluebell's] fur was fluffy and curiously luminous; but not too long, not bushy, like the fur of a vulgar Ritzy Persian. On the lawn before rain or in the early morning, she shone with a blue, unearthly light, while her eyes took on the vivid green of the grass. Curled on a chair indoors, she glowed mulberry-coloured. She always seemed to radiate from her small body some inward, spiritual colour. When she sat in the window on sunny days, her eyes were pure amber as they stared intently at outer space. I am sure she saw objects in space that I could not see. I never got used to Bluebell's loveliness. When I woke in the morning to see her sitting, a sheer Act of Praise, on my dressing-table, securely waiting for some life to happen, I would gaze at her with awe and with awe.[4]

Bluebell's miaow was music to her ears.

Bluebell soon settled down in the cottage ('like aristocrats, [cats] do not need stately homes') and Spark was her besotted admirer.

> If I were not a Christian, I would worship the Cat. The ancient Egyptians did so with much success. But at least it seems evident to me that the domestic cat is the aristocrat of the animal kingdom, occupying a place of quality in the Great Chain of Being second only to our aspiring, agitated and ever evolving selves.[5]

She found Bluebell's purr wonderfully comforting. Upon looking up 'purr' in the *Encyclopedia Britannica*, she was astonished to discover that a cat's purr could indicate either pleasure or pain. 'I don't remember any time when a cat of mine purred in pain', she later reflected. 'I wonder if other cat owners have had any such experience?'[6] To Spark, Bluebell's purr was a sign of supreme contentment.

Bluebell loved to perch on windowsills and watch birds outside ('you know cats do love birds', Muriel insisted once; 'they love to fondle them'[7]). The cat was also keen on catching butterflies. She came when called, although not invariably, and seemed to enter into Spark's moods: 'She would brood comically over my wrongs, and on occasions of rejoicing she quickly caught the spirit of the thing, sometimes taking a silly turn, leaping high, and landing with four legs outspread like a wonky new-born lamb. There was no end to Bluebell's virtues.'[8] Co-habitation was, it seems, beneficial to both. Spark grew calmer, more satisfied with her Catholicism, surer of her own authorial abilities. Watching, listening to and caring for Bluebell were entirely beneficial.

Tetchy at taking criticism from anyone else, Muriel Spark was able to accept Bluebell's strictures with gratitude. The cat, in her opinion, was a talented clairvoyant, gifted with ESP when it came to literature. 'She would sit on my manuscripts if what I had written was any good, but if she stepped over the notebooks with her fastidious pads, I knew there was something wrong with the stuff.'[9] Bluebell helped the process of literary creation by her mere presence. 'If you want to concentrate deeply on some problem', Spark advised other writers in her novel *A Far Cry from Kensington*,

> and especially some piece of writing or paper-work, you should acquire a cat. Alone with the cat in the room where you work ... the cat will invariably get up on your desk and settle placidly under the desk lamp ... the cat will settle down and be serene, with a serenity that passes all understanding. And the tranquillity of the cat will gradually come to affect you, sitting there at your desk, so that all the excitable qualities that impede your concentration compose themselves and give your mind back the self-command it has lost. You need not watch the cat all the time. Its presence alone is enough. The effect of a cat on your concentration is remarkable, very mysterious.[10]

Bluebell was always permitted to curl up on the pages of writing on Spark's desk, and Spark's own approach to writing grew positively cat-like in the process of thus sharing her desk. After collecting all her facts and ideas, she would then 'pounce' on her manuscript, picking up her fountain pen and writing with avidity.

In 1955 Muriel and Bluebell moved back to London and settled in a ground-floor flat at 13 Baldwin Crescent, Camberwell. When Muriel attended literary dinner parties, she carefully wrapped and brought home left-overs for Bluebell. Even when there was money for little else, Bluebell was always well fed. But when Muriel hosted parties, Bluebell made herself scarce – she was no party animal!

Muriel Spark spent hours simply reverencing her cat: 'I cannot speak highly enough of the cat, its casual freedom of spirit, its aloof anarchism and its marvellous beauty.'[11] She admired feline intelligence, but asserted that 'with cats, as with all true aristocrats, intelligence is not the main thing; they do not need brains, since they have felicity.'[12] She constantly revelled in Bluebell's looks: 'she was delicate in health and of small dimensions; she had no rival for wit and understanding; she glowed before rain with a blue unearthly light; she was a gifted clairvoyante ... leaped for joy at good news ... I have never seen her equal for catness, charm and radiance.'[13] 'Charming' was one of Muriel Spark's favourite adjectives – she never bestowed the word lightly on any creature, so it's a measure of her adoration of Bluebell that she used 'charm' to describe her.

Unsurprisingly, Spark soon began to celebrate her cat in her writings. Her poem 'Bluebell among the Sables' depicts the animal attacking the furs of an elegant lady visitor. Sables are costly and the visitor is understandably alarmed when her furs 'creep' as the animal moves stealthily within them. 'My God! My Sables!' she shrieks. But Muriel, narrative voice of the poem, quickly reassures her guest. 'No need for alarm', she says calmly, 'Those dead pelts can't cause Bluebell any harm.' Of course, the visitor is immediately wrong-footed. 'Poor soul, this put her in the wrong; / As one who somehow fails the higher vision.' She protests that her sables 'cost the earth', stroking her furs, while the poet strokes her cat. 'And all came even.' With delight, Spark watched her cat 'pummelling the sables', which seemed to glow as a result of this attention. In this unusual poem the live cat invigorates the inert furs by 'plying / The sensuous fabric with her shining pads'.[14] This poetic version of Bluebell appears to represent the artistic spirit, the feline spark of creativity that was within Muriel herself.

*The Informed Air*, a volume of essays published after Muriel Spark's death, contains 'Ailourophilia', a paean to Bluebell. She explains the unusual title for this essay about the cat: 'The Greeks, observing its fearful symmetry in motion, called the cat *ailouros* – a wave of the sea. Nothing restores the soul so much as the contemplation of a cat. In repose, it is like a lotus leaf. Its contentment is mystical.'[15] Undoubtedly, Spark was an ailurophile, a lover of cats.

Bluebell's namesake appears in Spark's second novel, *Robinson*, published in 1958, the year of the animal's untimely death. It's an odd novel about castaways on an island owned by a man named Robinson (the island is also called Robinson), and is Spark's version of *Robinson Crusoe*. She obviously felt that any castaway's lot would be vastly improved by feline companionship, so adds a cat called Bluebell to the plot. This Bluebell is also a 'little fluffy blue-grey cat'.[16] The narrator of the tale, January Marlow, teaches the animal to play ping-pong: 'to teach a cat to play ping-pong, you have to first win the confidence and approval of the cat.'[17] Some time in her past, January had taught a male cat the game, but she finds this second attempt more successful. Muriel Spark wrote the ping-pong episode from what sounds like experience – she must have taught Bluebell how to play, as she provides exact and detailed instructions. First, January Marlow plays other games with the creature to gain its confidence, hiding behind paper, miaowing and even whistling ('The Bluebells of Scotland' is, appropriately, a favourite tune). Once the cat's attention has been fully engaged, the ping-pong can start. 'After that I began daily to play with her, sometimes throwing the ping-pong ball in the air. She often leapt beautifully and caught it in her forepaws.'[18] Next, January places an old carton on end against a wall. Cats adore boxes, so Bluebell is swift to sit inside. The ball is sent into the box, bouncing against the cardboard, while Bluebell bats it with her paws and sends it flying back to January. She even uses her hind legs 'most comically',[19] or dribbles the ball across the patio with a footballer's skill. The book's Bluebell loves the game, waiting after lunch for the daily session, her mistress encouraging her performance with leonine growls. But Robinson is not impressed. He forcefully picks up the cat and takes her off to deal with a mouse in the barn. A ping-pong-playing cat is definitely a rarity in literature – Muriel Spark surely drew on personal experience in creating this scene. At the end of *Robinson*, January, rescued from the island, which is starting to sink into the sea, is offered the cat by Robinson and takes Bluebell home to Chelsea. In this novel about evil, distrust and suspicion, Bluebell's is the only happy personality within its pages.

In 1961 Spark's masterpiece *The Prime of Miss Jean Brodie* was published. There's no cat in the story of the teacher and her pupils, but the heroine, Jean Brodie, has definite feline qualities. Self-absorbed, immaculately groomed and elegant, mysterious about her past, Miss Brodie, like a cat, is chary about bestowing her favours. The cat's traditional liking for cream is given a sardonic twist in the novel when Miss Brodie obsesses about her group of schoolgirls, who are the 'crème de la crème'.

In 1992 Spark published *Curriculum Vitae*, a vivid account of the people and places who inspired her work. She wrote of her parents, other writers who inspired her, her old school and the teacher who was the model for Miss Brodie, and she also wrote about her cat. There are fewer than thirty photographs included in the book, but the last one is of Bluebell, more evidence of how important she was in Muriel's life.

Muriel Spark liked to review cat books, and had strong views on what they should contain: 'Sensible cat books are devoted to praising the cat for its catness',[20] she declared. It was the essential qualities of the animal that she so loved, and that she often emulated in her own life.

Bluebell was only four years old when she began to sicken. Spark was frantic with worry and vets were consulted. Bluebell bore their ministrations patiently, but to no avail. The vet announced that the cat should be 'put to sleep'. Spark, like most good authors, liked exactitude in words – she was having none of such talk. 'You mean you want to put her to death', she responded. The vet tried again: 'Oh I wouldn't put it that way', he protested. But

Spark insisted that the man simply wanted to kill her cat. The inevitable couldn't be postponed. After six distressing weeks, she admitted that her beloved companion (she hated calling Bluebell her pet, convinced she was a domesticated animal and an equal, not a creature she owned) would have to be killed. Watching her suffer was agonizing. In August 1958 the 'Gestapo' arrived. 'In came the hired assassins, carrying between them a metal box, Bluebell's gas chamber.'[21] Although asked to leave, she was reluctant, certain that Bluebell needed her, but she was firmly 'put out of the room'. Four minutes later, she was called back in, to view her dead cat. Then Bluebell's body was unceremoniously 'dumped in a sack' and taken away.

Much as she loved her cat, Muriel Spark was first and foremost a writer, and nothing could stop her authorial eye from observing, unsentimentally, all the raw details of the death – the rigidity of the once active paws, the stinking pus in Bluebell's ear, and then the cat's poor eyes, 'upturned, wildly staring, glazed amber'.[22] She wrote letters to friends describing Bluebell's death unemotionally. Yet it's a measure of her pain that she was unable ever to turn the tragedy into ironic comedy, her usual way of dealing with trauma. Bluebell's death could only ever be tragic. She complained that loving something with such a short lifespan was a cruel arrangement and vowed never again to make herself emotionally vulnerable by loving a cat.

Famous last words! Cats had an indestructible hold on Muriel Spark. She resisted for a while when friends tried gifting her another kitten, but before long other cats entered her life, though none would ever attain the status of Bluebell in her heart. In the 1960s she moved to Rome. On Easter Monday 1967 she encountered a stray, who soon shared her home, sat on her manuscripts and even played with them, just as Bluebell had done. This cat was named Pasquetta. Soon Pasquetta was joined by Spider, who came to her from fellow novelist and cat lover Patricia Highsmith, who was leaving Italy to return to England. The two writers never met, but they bonded over Spider and corresponded for years, in letters filled with Spider queries and details. Spider remained with her until his death in 1973, when Spark wrote: 'You could tell he had been a writer's cat. He would sit by me, seriously, as I wrote, while all my other cats filtered away.'[23]

It was in Rome that she met sculptor Penelope Jardine, who became a close friend and companion for Muriel's last decades. Penelope gave Muriel the emotional stability she craved, but she still needed felines – and Penelope was a fellow ailurophile. The two women settled in Tuscany and soon their home had cat residents galore. At one time there were seven cats – Baby Dave, Lucy, Frankie, Aurora, One-Eyed Riley, Little Grey and Miss Fisher. Benji and Little Miss Blackberry were two other strays to whom they offered shelter. All were supposed to be outdoor cats, but they soon slunk inside. It's a pity they were not solely indoor animals, because rural Tuscany held many perils for them. There were snakes in the grass, while local hunters, wanting to ensure the repopulation of the local wildlife after each hunting season, laid out poison for cats and dogs. This cruel practice caused the deaths of several of Muriel and Penelope's dogs and also some of their cats. Muriel protested publicly against such cruelty, but there was little she could do to stop it. One awful day Aurora came home dragging a wire cage caught in her fur. Muriel's last cat was Pinot Grigio, a stripey black and white cat, another stray. He had the honour of appearing in the photograph of Dame Muriel Spark which accompanied her 2006 obituary in *The Times*.

Muriel Spark believed in an afterlife, though was convinced it would not suit her long-term. Perhaps the Heaven she believed in would have had greater permanent appeal could she have been certain that Bluebell would meet her at the Pearly Gates, winding her sinuous body around Muriel's legs? Bluebell was the cat who charmed, comforted and inspired her. She could not speak highly enough of this adored animal. In 'Ailourophilia' she stated: 'To my mind, the flower and consummation of the species was my late cat, Bluebell, short of whose perfection every other cat in history and literature inevitably falls.'[24] High praise indeed.

PAWS FOR THOUGHT
# The cat who helped children learn to read

The *Dick and Jane* primers were just not working! American schoolchildren were slipping behind in their reading and the bland, repetitive stories about Dick and Jane were simply not grabbing attention or sparking interest in the printed word. Dr Seuss (Theodor Geisel) had already written a quirky tale about an elephant named Horton when he was asked by an educational publisher to write something entertaining that might help kids learn their letters. Dr Seuss's response was *The Cat in the Hat*, published in 1957.

Given a list of simple and familiar words, he decided to create a story based on the first two rhyming words he found. Those happened to be 'cat' and 'hat'. The book was an instant commercial and critical success, and literacy rates began improving. Kids loved the anarchic cat who enters the house while Mum is out, causes total mayhem while watched by Sally and her brother, then rapidly tidies up and disappears. Within a few years the book had sold over a million copies and *Dick and Jane* primers left American classrooms for good. Dr Seuss claimed that the achievement of which he was most proud was causing the 'death' of those boring books.

The legacy of that cat in his red and white striped hat is remarkable. His appearance led to the creation of Beginner Books, a publishing firm centred on books for those learning to read. The famous cat has appeared on stage, in musicals, cartoons, film and television, on postage stamps and in the media. *The Cat in the Hat* continues to appeal. In 2020 it was placed second on the New York Public Library's list of 'Top Ten Checkouts of All Time'.

# EL MAGNIFICO
## who enchanted Doris Lessing

*El Magnifico condescended to live with
Doris Lessing, born in Kermanshah, Iran, in
1919, died in London in 2013, novelist, winner
of the 2007 Nobel Prize for Literature.*

A friend once recalled Doris Lessing as having 'a cat-like kind of charm – a wary, cool, feline sort of quality'.[1] Perhaps that was why she related so well to cats throughout her long life. As a girl, she considered becoming a vet. Fortunately for literature, she changed her mind and turned to writing instead, but she was always a nurse to injured cats, a devoted feeder of strays, and she opened her London home to any feline in need of shelter, so her veterinary ambitions found amateur scope, if not professional.

Doris Lessing grew up in Rhodesia (now Zimbabwe). As a child she was intrigued by the semi-feral cats on her parents' farm. Her African home was a harsh place for cats – once she watched horrified as a hawk swooped down, then flew off with a kitten in its talons. The tiny creature 'vanished mewing into the sky'.[2] Her mother, also a cat lover, fired her shotgun, but it was no use – the kitten was gone. The Tayler family (Lessing was the name of her second husband) had cats as pets, but maintaining a border between tame and wild was challenging. Wild cats mated with domestic cats, or lured them away to a life of crime, raiding fowl-runs and living rough. Doris's mother once shot a cat she mistook for a snake, and one day Doris watched, terrified, as a cat and a snake engaged in a wary standoff lasting some hours (in the end, neither creature was harmed). The nearest vet was in Salisbury (now Harare), 70 miles away; any doctoring had to be done at the farm, and there was little chance of taking cats to be spayed or neutered, resulting in numerous litters. Most kittens had to be drowned, an awful job stoically performed by Mrs Tayler. One year, however, she went on strike and refused to drown more kittens. The result was a positive infestation of cats marauding around the property. Doris and her father tried using chloroform, but found the method inefficient, so he simply got his gun and shot them. The 'holocaust of cats'[3] sickened them both.

Lessing's first real love affair with a cat occurred when she was eleven. The object of her devotion was a bluish-grey Persian, with green eyes. He fell into a tub of hot water, developed pneumonia as a result, and died. She never forgot his 'rough, trembling'[4] voice in his last moments and vowed then and there that never again would she make herself so vulnerable to grief. He was '*the* Cat never to be replaced'.[5] For twenty-five years she kept that resolution.

Her life over the next two decades was decidedly unsettled – two husbands, children that were born and left in the care of others, a move to London, a variety of jobs and several rented flats. Lessing knew cats need a settled home, and wouldn't be happy joining her peripatetic life. But in the 1950s she was living in Earl's Court and had a rodent infestation – she needed a good mouser. So, she obtained a half-grown black and white female but, still protecting herself emotionally, remained determined not to fall in love with this new arrival. The new cat was incredibly fussy – lightly cooked calves' liver (done in butter) or lightly boiled whiting were what she expected for dinner. Although Lessing did try to starve her into submission, she was the one who eventually cracked and fed her cat what was demanded. When a litter of kittens was born on the kitchen floor, they too only ate what their mother ate. And she proved a useless mouser. She had to be put down after falling from the roof. Lessing grieved, but not deeply.

By the 1960s Lessing was once again living in a cat-friendly neighbourhood. Visiting friends told her about their new part-Siamese kitten. They were newly married, but the kitten enjoyed pressing itself against the husband and getting in the way whenever the couple grew amorous. The wife was starting to feel she was losing the love of her life to a cat, just like the wife in Colette's *La Chatte*. The solution was to give the kitten to Lessing. The kitten was six weeks old, delicate and enchanting, grey-cream in colour, with yellow eyes and a smoky Siamese front. Grey Cat, as she unimaginatively came to be called,[6] was a timid animal, snuggling right down in Doris's bed, under all the blankets. However, as she gained confidence she fought neighbouring cats and grew lusty. All the local toms were interested and Grey Cat was soon pregnant. In Lessing's opinion she was too young for pregnancy, and indeed she proved to be a poor mother. After her third litter she was spayed. Lessing, whose own sexuality was deeply important to her, felt she'd betrayed her pet by turning her into 'a spinster cat'.[7]

Soon a little black cat joined the household; but Black Cat was always subservient to Grey. Lessing delighted in her rich blackness: 'She is black, black, black ... not a white hair anywhere.'[8] When the cat got enteritis, Doris had a real fight to keep her alive, forcing liquid into her and rubbing warmth into her stiff body. Black Cat recovered. Lessing took both cats to her Devon cottage for holidays; but their persistent catching of birds always distressed her.

Over the next years, various cats came and went. There was Rufus, a shabby orange stray who followed her home one day. He had kidney problems and was 'an old derelict'[9] when she took him in, but he became an important member of her family and she wrote about him in *Rufus the Survivor*.

Rufus had to learn to live with Charles, a tabby. And there were feline visitors – one named The Pirate made regular and voracious food raids. Doris always left water bowls out in summer for thirsty local strays. Rufus had 'the intelligence'[10] of the survivor and soon adapted to sharing the Lessing home with other cats. His health problems continued – an ulcer on his ear, teeth falling out, more kidney problems – but Doris nursed him through it all.

Doris Lessing's last cat, and the one she loved most of all, was El Magnifico. He arrived in 1983 when one of her cats, Susie, gave birth to seven kittens. Susie had been living rough, was tired and scared and had happily accepted shelter with Lessing. She showed little interest in her kittens, but somehow six survived. One of those was a black and white scrap, slightly bigger than his siblings. When Lessing inspected the blanket full of kittens in her kitchen, this tiny creature immediately climbed up her leg and body, right to her chin. There it cuddled in, purring. 'This was love, and for life',[11] Doris asserted. Once again, she'd given her heart to a cat. As the largest of the litter, the kitten was soon bossing his siblings and doing his mother's job for her. When she had further litters he assisted by licking the newborns and carrying them around.

El Magnifico took some time to be matched to the right name. As nursery tyrant, he was at first called Butch. Lessing saw that as only a temporary name, and over the months it morphed into Butchkin, Pushkin, Pusskin, Pusscat and Pushka. For a while he was even General Pinknose the Third, and General Butchkin. But when El Magnifico was finally thought of, the name fitted perfectly. 'El Magnifico suits him best, suits him because he truly is such a magnificent cat',[12] she insisted. In 2008 she told the *Wall Street Journal* that 'the cat I communicated with best was El Magnifico. He was such a clever cat. We used to have sessions when we tried to be on each other's level. He knew we were trying. When push came to shove, though, the communication was pretty limited.'[13] She knew that her cat kept 'the lonely stalk'[14] of the leopard or panther and would always remain a creature of the jungle in his independent aloofness.

El Magnifico was extremely handsome, a 'lordly beast',[15] with dramatic black and white colouring which she described as 'harlequinade'.[16] All Lessing's visitors commented on his good looks. She was enchanted by his beauty: 'Delicious cat! Exquisite cat! Satiny cat! Cat like a soft owl, cat with paws like moths, jewelled cat, miraculous cat! Cat, cat, cat, cat!'[17] He was too proud to compete with her other cats. Rufus tried hard to be 'top cat', but El Magnifico made sure Rufus failed. He ruled the household and nobody could forget it. He was a beast with intuitive intelligence. He permitted Lessing to join him in 'a duet of mutual admiration'.[18] When other cats got sick, he coughed too – Lessing soon found this was a sympathy-gaining ploy, and not for any medical reason (he was briefly known as Sir Laurence Olivier Butchkin as a result of such acting skills). He draped himself over her typewriter to 'encourage' her work. She spent hours at her bedroom window, looking down on the garden where El Magnifico ruled, watching his antics. He slept in her bed at the top of the house, ate neatly and moderately, and thrilled her with his repertoire of purrs and mews. When Lessing woke each morning, there was El Magnifico walking up the bed to her, and falling back to sleep in her arms. He liked being brushed, kneaded and massaged, and when they sat together Lessing knew he demanded her full attention – no absent-minded stroking would satisfy this cat.

When he was fourteen, El Magnifico developed a lump on his shoulder. He had been to the vet to be neutered when young, and had found it traumatizing; nevertheless another visit was clearly required. The vet delivered bad news – El Magnifico had bone cancer. Lessing believed an operation might give him a few more years and so a decision was taken to remove one front leg, haunch and shoulder. He had lived his entire life in one house, so going to the vet was disturbing, even without a major operation. El Magnifico was deprived of food before surgery, given injections, and a large patch of rich black fur was shaved off. Lessing lovingly caressed the paw and leg that would soon be gone, and left her darling to the ministrations of the vet. She phoned frantically several times a day to check on his progress. He came through well, but after a few days of post-operative care was pining for Lessing and home.

El Magnifico came home deeply shocked. Sore, weak and groggy, betrayed by those who he'd thought loved him, he wanted desperately to escape outdoors where freedom awaited. As Lessing carried him upstairs, he suddenly leapt from her arms, 'flung himself down all seven flights of stairs, rolling, falling, jumping, getting down them any way he could',[19] and crept into his garden sanctuary.

Lessing's father had lost a leg as a result of war injury, so she assumed her cat could slowly adapt to missing a limb. And he did. Soon El Magnifico had conquered the stairs and could climb onto the bed, but his pride had been deeply hurt and his confidence was never quite the same. Occasionally he miscalculated his 'lordly careless stroll'[20] and fell on his nose. His remaining front leg swelled because of the extra weight it had to bear, and toileting necessitated more careful balancing. But the operation gave El Magnifico at least three extra years.

During those years he was an 'only cat' in Lessing's home. He missed the feline companions with whom he had once contended for pecking order and rights. He'd call for his lost friends in the garden, flirt with the female next door (she disdained the overtures of this aged, disabled suitor) and he spent more and more time on a low sofa, near the radiator. The stairs grew too arduous and Lessing missed his yellow eyes in the night. She helped him keep clean, because a one-paw job couldn't achieve the same results, gently cleaning his ears and washing his eyes. El Magnifico grew stiff with age. Lessing lavished him with loving attention: 'What a luxury a cat is', she enthused. 'The moments of shocking and startling pleasure in a day, the feel of the beast, the soft sleekness under your palm, the warmth when you wake on a cold night, the grace and charm even in a quite ordinary workaday puss.'[21] But she lamented her inability to know his mind – was he suffering pain, what treatment would help? She even wondered whether wild cats should ever have been domesticated.

Slowly El Magnifico weakened and then, quietly, he passed away. She never wanted another cat. Once again her heart was broken at the loss of this adored feline friend. The greatest tribute Doris Lessing could pay to her beloved was to write about him. She did this with brilliant visual detail, truth and simplicity, and with the eye of someone who has closely observed cats all her life. El Magnifico was immortalized by a great writer – not many cats can claim that. Her greatest tribute to him was in the story *The Old Age of El Magnifico*. It tells the tale of this awkwardly loveable cat and his struggles to cope without a leg. Lessing writes movingly and sympathetically of the plight of the disabled. The book came out as a little hardback gift edition.

In 2007 Doris Lessing won the Nobel Prize for Literature. Many of her writings mention cats and some are exclusively cat books. *Particularly Cats*, an account of the cats who had shared her life, includes anecdotes about El Magnifico (at the time of writing still known as Butchkin). This was published in 1967. *Rufus the Survivor* appeared in 1993, and *The Old Age of El Magnifico* in 2000. The three stories were combined in a 2002 omnibus edition as *On Cats*. Unsurprisingly, other novels and stories feature cats. In the 1972 short story 'An Old Woman and her Cat' Hetty Pennefather lives a hard life in a council flat after working for years as a rag trader. Her children are ashamed of her; she has lost touch with friends; and her only companion is Tibby, her tom cat. He catches pigeons, which she can cook. Loyal and loving, he warms her at night. When the council introduces new rules banning pets from their accommodation, Hetty faces a hard choice. This poignant, tragic tale is an indictment of the way in which older people can be treated by the authorities. It is a story in which the consoling power of a cat is made manifest in an unsentimental way.

Doris Lessing was not an easy woman – prickly, a natural loner, an extremely poor mother and an unfaithful wife, she seems to have found cats much easier than people. A former assistant wrote of her: 'Doris just doesn't deal with human beings very well. She deals with cats very well.'[22] Cats never disappointed or caused her irritation.

Most of her important childhood memories did not concern her family, but rather the cats she had watched and loved. Cats gave her company, consoled her in times of stress, endlessly fascinated her, inspired her writing, and brought out her best side. Human beings were just too difficult, but she was always available to respond to the needs of a cat. 'People don't purr',[23] Doris Lessing once joked. She was happiest with her cats.

## PAWS FOR THOUGHT
### Socks, the letter-writing cat

Some cats of authors even have their own postbags. Socks, the black and white cat who permitted Bill and Hillary Clinton to share the White House with him, received more letters than did the president. Socks, a stray, was adopted by the Clintons in 1991, after he jumped into the arms of their daughter Chelsea. He was named Socks for his white paws and was soon famous. Sometimes Socks visited schools or hospitals; his face was placed on the White House website, and soon he had his own web page. Socks, however, was not happy sharing the presidential mansion – when Buddy the Labrador arrived as a bouncing puppy in 1997, Socks was not impressed. Bill Clinton spent much of his time in office trying to resolve conflicts in the Middle East, but was never able to resolve the conflict between his pets. When the Clintons left the White House in 2001, Buddy went with them, but Socks was left in the care of the secretary. Socks died from cancer in 2009.

In 1998 Hillary Clinton published a book featuring some of the letters American children had sent the White House pets. In *Dear Socks, Dear Buddy: Kids' Letters to the First Pets* Socks was asked which of the Clintons he liked the best, whether he was allowed to watch MTV, and about his rivalry with Buddy. Proceeds from the book benefited the National Park Foundation.

Did Socks try and assist when Governor Clinton and Senator Gore wrote *Putting People First: How We Can All Change America* or *Between Hope and History* as part of their election campaign? Was Socks allowed free rein in the Oval Office once Clinton became president?

Socks received sacks of mail. Sometimes the letters came from other cats, asking enviously about his White House comforts. Requests for paw-autographed photos of himself were common, along with thousands of questions about his diet, habits and preferences. Socks was a well-mannered cat so letters were always answered. This annoyed Republican representative Dan Burton, who argued that White House stationery and stamps should not be used in correspondence with a cat.

A White House cat seems a very good idea – one can only hope that there will be more of them.

# WOOSKIT
## who morphed into Slinky Malinki for Dame Lynley Dodd

*Wooskit condescended to live with Dame Lynley Dodd, children's book author and illustrator, born in Rotorua, New Zealand, in 1941, currently living in Tauranga, New Zealand.*

'EEEEEOWWWFFTZ!'[1] Scarface Claw's greeting to Hairy Maclary and his friends, as they turn a corner and meet him unexpectedly, is the only line of dialogue in the book, and what a fabulous one it is! What parent, reading the story aloud, can resist putting expression into that wonderful 'cat-cophany' of vowels and consonants? What child could fail to delight in the glorious hissing and spitting of that made-up word? When Lynley Dodd impersonated Scarface Claw on Australian radio, her rendition of this vivid line nearly killed someone's pet cockatoo – it keeled over in shock at hearing the awful noise.

It's a memorably dramatic entrance for a cat who has become a globally loved character of children's literature. The accompanying drawing, with Scarface rearing up to confront the intruders, whiskers quivering, teeth bared menacingly, is very cleverly done. Lynley Dodd loves the novels of Jane Austen[2] and credits her as an influence on her own work. Jane Austen once wrote 'An artist cannot do anything slovenly';[3] Lynley Dodd has followed that advice to the full. Her texts and illustrations are painstakingly thought out, superbly crafted and revised, so every detail is right. And it's thanks to her own personal knowledge of cats and dogs that she is able to get exactly right her portrayals of Scarface Claw, Slinky Malinki, Hairy Maclary and his canine friends, who are today so loved by the reading public.

An only child, growing up in a huge pine forest in the middle of New Zealand's North Island, far from any town, really ought to have felt lonely, but young Lynley Weeks (she became Lynley Dodd when she married Tony Dodd in 1965) knew great love from her parents, felt secure in her home and had the rich world of her imagination to sustain her. Fairy stories, Enid Blyton and lots of magazines provided characters and tales to dream over. She loved Felix the Cat, while Dr Seuss's books became great favourites, and later an inspiration. But even better than fictional cats were the cats in her own home: not only the family's own two pussies, but visiting ones as well.

When she was about six years old, her family acquired Squib, inherited – name and all – from the people who'd been running the Rangataiki Hotel, but wanted to leave the district. Squib was a large tabby who bore the marks of many battles – scars on his nose, nicks out of his ears, and a leg stiffened from traumatic encounters with traps (probably laid for possums, an introduced pest in New Zealand). It was almost as if he had a wooden leg, so stiff had it become from the damage of gin traps. But lameness never stopped Squib from doing what he did best. Squib terrorized the neighbourhood; no visiting cat was safe from his menaces – they'd be rapidly 'seen off' by this ferocious cat. However, Squib had a secret and the Weeks family knew what it was. He was, at heart, utterly soppy. Lynley could dress him in doll's clothes, tuck him into a toy bed, and he was always happy to be petted and stroked. 'He would have been mortified if his enemies had ever found out what a softie he was at home',[4] she recorded. Outdoors he changed personality – there he had a reputation for ferocity which had to be maintained. Two-sided Squib was straight out of Stevenson's novella *Dr Jekyll and Mr Hyde*.

It was Squib who was the model for Scarface Claw, 'the toughest tom in town'.[5] Scarface is king of his neighbourhood – he taunts the dogs from on high, his battered ears tell of past battles, he takes positive delight in scaring other animals, and he is memorably afraid of absolutely nothing at all, except his own reflection in a mirror. Scarface does occasionally have to submit to human assistance – he gets rescued from the roof of a car; when he finds himself unaccountably stuck up a tree, people have to bring him down. When he enters a pet competition, he wins 'Worst Temper' award with no effort. Children love Scarface Claw: he provides menace and scariness in just the right proportions; his yellow eyes gleam wickedly from the illustrations; and young readers love spotting Scarface lurking in wait for Hairy Maclary, or creeping from behind a sofa to threaten a row of contented pussies ranged before the fire.

After Squib departed this world in 1951, other cats could move in to the Weeks' residence. 'In my Kaingaroa Forest childhood, it was understood by local catdom that all roads led to our house. Proof of this came one freezing morning when my father had to step over nine cats in two sleeping piles on our porch doormats. Only two of the nine were ours.'[6] One of them was Owlie, a tawny part-Persian, who went walkabout for two years to have adventures, then returned and stayed for the rest of his life. There were dogs too – felines and canines coexisted happily in the Weeks' home as Lynley made her way through school and began developing her love of drawing. At first it was princesses or gorgeous brides that she sketched, but Sean, the family's dachshund, was soon serving as a model and she sketched him sleeping in a little box (Sean was later reincarnated as Schnitzel von Krumm, and his box became the dog's tatty yet beloved basket in *Schnitzel von Krumm's Basketwork*). Dogs, ducks, birds, turtles and, of course, cats soon featured regularly in her sketchbooks. She attended art school in Auckland, trained as a teacher, worked and married, but never dreamed of becoming a famous author.

Fortunately, her husband Tony Dodd also loved cats, and so Wooskit was welcomed into their lives in 1968. Lynley, expecting a baby, had just finished teaching art at Queen Margaret College. Her son Matthew arrived soon after Wooskit. He was an SPCA rescue cat and stood out from among the other cats there, because he looked up at the Dodds with eyes that said 'I'll come home with you!'[7] A small, black, noisy kitten, soon he was ruling the roost. Oddly for someone who so delights in creating memorable names, Lynley struggled with naming the new pet. For a long time he was just 'puss cat', but gradually that evolved into Wooskit. He was, as described by Tony, 'a standard black SPCA dustbin cat'.[8] Sleek and full of character, with a kink at the end of his very long tail and with two white patches on chest and stomach, Wooskit showed a passion for boxes, cupboards, paper bags and unusual hiding places. He also liked long walks, hiking into the hills with Lynley and Tony.

It was Wooskit's love of hiding that helped bring Lynley Dodd into print. In 1972 she teamed up with Tony's relative Eve Sutton, a freelance writer in New Zealand. The women had once discussed collaborating on a book, with Eve writing and Lynley illustrating, but family life intervened and nothing had come of the project. Out of the blue, Eve reminded Lynley of their idea and insisted they set about it. By now Lynley had a daughter, Elizabeth, as well as a son, so spent a lot of time reading to her children. Consequently, she loved the idea of a picture book for new readers. When Eve asked for possible topics, Lynley immediately thought of her Wooskit: 'the only thing I can think of is our crazy cat who climbs in and out of boxes and cupboards'.[9] The result was *My Cat Likes to Hide in Boxes* and Wooskit was the model for her illustrations, although he was not given his actual colour: 'I coloured him grey in those illustrations but quickly regretted it and have apologised to him ever since by giving him bit parts in several books[10] as his black and shiny self.'[11] Published in 1973, the book was an immediate success and won New Zealand's Esther Glen Medal for junior fiction. Lynley Dodd was thrilled to be handed her award by none other than her hero, Dr Seuss. Wooskit achieved stardom as the box-loving cat. His picture appeared in *New Zealand Woman's Weekly*, showing him perched happily atop a dog food box. While her illustrating style evolved over the next years, Lynley had essentially found her formula – animals, catchy rhymes, repetition and vivid pictures. She produced two more books in the 1970s: *The Nickle Nackle Tree* and *Titimus Trim*. *The Apple Tree* and *The Smallest Turtle* followed in the early 1980s. *Hairy Maclary from Donaldson's Dairy* made its debut in 1983 and was an instant success, rapidly followed by more fabulous tales featuring the scruffy dog and his friends: *Hairy Maclary's Bone*, *Hairy Maclary Scattercat*, *Hairy Maclary's Caterwaul Caper* and *Hairy Maclary's Rumpus at the Vet*.

Wooskit had to wait some years for a starring role as his own recognizable self. *Slinky Malinki* was published in 1990. Like Scarface Claw, he has 'bright yellow eyes'[12] and leads a secret life. Slinky is essentially a burglar. On nighttime prowls he raids houses, pilfering sausages, bandages, pencils and even old socks. Children love the medley of objects that naughty Slinky brings home. He drags the assorted items to 'his house on the hill',[13] but then trouble starts. Glue spills, the strands from an unravelling jersey tangle his legs, a clock falls and chimes madly, and Slinky's family is woken by the hubbub. When Slinky is branded a 'criminal cat!'[14] by his horrified family, there's a wonderful image of dishevelled Slinky, his puzzled look proclaiming total ignorance of the mess, his whiskers gummed up with leaking glue. Slinky's thieving has to end, and from that time he stays home, whiskers nicely adjusted, resisting the siren call of further midnight raids. Wooskit gained literary immortality in his role as the fabulous and memorable Slinky Malinki.

But Slinky's feline career had only just begun. *Slinky Malinki, Open the Door*; *Slinky Malinki Catflaps*; *Slinky Malinki's Christmas Crackers*; and *Slinky Malinki, Early Bird* gave him further misadventures. Wooskit/Slinky has won awards; his deeds have been translated into many other languages; he has appeared in art exhibitions, on stage and television; and he has helped Lynley gain honorary degrees and become Dame Lynley Dodd. Millions of copies of the books have been sold around the world. These are no mean achievements for Wooskit, a dustbin cat from the SPCA.

Unlike Scarface Claw, Slinky Malinki makes friends. There's Stickybeak Syd the parrot; the marmalade tabby Butterball Brown; wide-eyed cat Greywacke Jones, who endures Scarface Claw's terrorizing attentions; tigerish Grizzly MacDuff; elegant Pimpernel Pugh; the fluffy bombshell that is Mushroom Magee; and the darling quartet of Poppadum kittens, who move and play together en masse. When Lynley was a girl, she and her father made a game of inventing amusing, ridiculous names. Neither could have dreamed that the game would eventually prove so useful. There's such charm in the fantastic, euphonious names Lynley Dodd bestows on her fictional felines.

Slinky Malinki is now immortal, but sadly Wooskit used up his nine lives and died, aged thirteen, in 1981. There were other cats who condescended to live with the Dodds – Sam and Pipi, brother and sister kittens who were born under a flax bush in the garden of her parents' Mt Maunganui home. Much to the relief of Mr and Mrs Weeks, Lynley and Tony took the tabby and black kittens home to Lower Hutt. Sam, not the brightest of cats, spent hours under the bird table, hoping something feathered would fall within paw-reach, while Pipi was rather timid, though still capable of tussling with her brother. Tony retired and the Dodds moved to Tauranga. Sam had died in 1990, but Pipi accompanied them and lived to be nineteen, well cared for by the whole family. Lynley sketched them, but they failed to enter any of her stories in their own characters.

The next arrival was Suu Kyi, named for Aung San Suu Kyi, Burmese diplomat, author and 1991 Nobel Peace Prize laureate.[15] Suu Kyi, who moved in with the Dodds in 2001, was a sealpoint Burmese, elegant and sleek. It was her penchant for destroying the family's Christmas tree which provided the plot for *Slinky Malinki's Christmas Crackers*: 'She would work her way up through the foliage, scattering baubles and tinsel in all directions, while she searched for her favourite decoration (a mouse with a hat, red nose and pipe cleaner tail).'[16] Suu Kyi was an early riser; her desire to rouse the family from slumber gave Lynley the idea for *Slinky Malinki, Early Bird*. While Suu Kyi was not the animal in the illustrations, she too played an important role in making Lynley Dodd's books the icons they have become. Suu Kyi had the disconcerting habit of leaping onto shoulders and draping herself there like a sleek fur stole. Visitors unused to the habit were taken aback when suddenly assailed by a Burmese cat. For the last four years of her life Suu Kyi was diabetic, needing daily injections. She died in 2018, aged seventeen, and was hugely missed. Currently Lynley Dodd's home is catless, but memories of her beloved cats live on in her books. Because she misses 'a warm furry cushion' on her lap, she is starting to think it might be 'time for another miaow at the door...'[17]

Children love encountering fictional favourites in forms other than the pages of a book. They can find Scarface Claw and Slinky Malinki, cast in bronze, at the Tauranga waterfront. The group of statues was commissioned by the arts body Creative Tauranga, while the New Zealand government supplied funding of $150,000. It was a way of honouring their local author (Lynley has lived in Tauranga since 1991). The design is by Swiss-born Brigitte Wuest, who went on to become head sculptor of Weta Workshop and designer for Peter Jackson's *Lord of the Rings* trilogy. Brigitte's children had grown up with Hairy Maclary books and she wanted to create a tactile work that children could climb over and run around. She had great fun turning 2D drawings into 3D sculptures and the result has been pleasing children and adults alike since it was erected in 2015. Scarface Claw perches triumphantly atop a pillar, gazing down at Hairy Maclary, Bitzer Maloney, Schnitzel von Krumm, Bottomley Potts and Muffin McLay, who attempt uselessly to reach him (Hercules Morse has sensibly given up and lain down), while Slinky Malinki slinks past, almost in the gutter, making the most of his canine enemies being distracted. The whole forms a charming storybook scene and is a superb tribute to an author whose animal creations have so enriched children's literature. There was considerable outrage a few years ago when a vandal kicked off Hairy Maclary's fabulously scruffy tail; he was filmed on a security camera at 3 a.m. doing the deed. Dog and tail have since been reunited.

Cats have always been a source of comfort, fun and inspiration to Lynley Dodd. She's the first to admit she's an animal person. While her art-school training and early artistic efforts were mostly focused on humans, sharing her life with cats and dogs gave her the idea of creating picture books about those animals. Many times over the years has she rushed for her sketch pad to record some silly, bizarre behaviour of one of her cats. One example is her sketch of Suu Kyi when a pair of drying knickers fell off a bathroom rail onto her head. Instead of rushing off in fright, she continued wearing the knickers, looking ridiculous with ears forming two peaks in the fabric.

Few of today's authors for children have become as rapidly beloved for their books as has Dame Lynley Dodd. Had New Zealand neighbours not been relocating and therefore sent Squib to her family, there might never have been a Scarface Claw to terrorize dogs, assert his authority and give children exactly the right mix of threat and thrills. And had there been no trip to the SPCA to rescue a kitten named Wooskit from a life of hardship, there would have been no 'fiendish and sly'[18] Slinky Malinki enjoying robbery and mayhem alongside the brilliant illustrations which charm us all. Lynley Dodd's books are Kiwi icons. She has enriched juvenile literature and celebrated the cats of her life in a memorable, visually stunning and truly marvellous way.

# TAILPIECE

Writers throughout history, in their lonely occupation, have turned to cats for comfort, inspiration and companionship. They have depicted cats in their poems and stories, plays and novels, and have celebrated the glory of cats, large and small, purebred and moggy, timid and bold, in their letters, essays and articles. The paw prints of the feline species have made a mark in literature.

What sort of writer shares his or her writing space with a cat? Is it a person who prefers to care for others (whereas those who get dogs perhaps prefer to receive affection)? Cats are certainly less trouble than dogs – they don't need 'walkies', rain or shine; their toilet habits are cleaner; they are generally cheaper to feed; quieter (a miaow is less noisy than a bark); and they don't bite the postman, who could be delivering acceptance letters from publishers. A cat can stimulate a writer's imagination and its elusive spirit can function as a symbol of the words and plots writers are trying so hard to pin down on the page. For many authors, dogs are too obvious, lacking subtlety, their indoor presence too boisterous and demanding. Cats seem to be just right. French writer Théophile Gautier commented that cats 'ramble round the house with their velvet footfalls, as the genius of the place; or come and seat themselves on the table near the writer companioning his thought, keeping company with his thoughts and watching him ... with intelligent tenderness and magical penetration'.[1] Cats can be intelligent literary critics, or even function as paperweights by sitting on a manuscript and keeping it anchored on a windy day. A cat's silent aura dispels loneliness; its graceful remoteness brings comfort and pleasure. Feline beauty and style provide a standard that authors can attempt to match in literary style. Baudelaire insisted of cats that 'their fecund loins of magic sparks are full'.[2]

Cats have condescended to enslave many wonderful writers: Louisa May Alcott, Kazim Ali, Isabel Allende, Kingsley Amis, Guillaume Apollinaire, Hiro Arikawa, Matthew Arnold, Margaret Atwood, W.H. Auden, Joanna Baillie, Honoré de Balzac, Charles Baudelaire, Samuel Beckett, Hilaire Belloc, Karen Blixen, Enid Blyton, Judy Blume, Jorge Luis Borges, James Bowen, Ray Bradbury, Lilian Jackson Braun, Emily Brontë, Helen Gurley Brown, William S. Burroughs, Samuel Butler, Albert Camus, Karel Čapek, Truman Capote, Thomas Carlyle, Angela Carter, Raymond Chandler, Anuja Chauhan, Anton Chekhov, Beverly Cleary, Jean Cocteau, Julio Cortázar,

Noël Coward, William Cowper, Robertson Davies, W.H. Davies, E.M. Delafield, Philip K. Dick, Lena Divani, Marguerite Duras, T.S. Eliot, Louise Erdrich, Zelda Fitzgerald, Gillian Flynn, Janet Frame, Anatole France, Anne Frank, William Faulkner, Neil Gaiman, André Gide, Allen Ginsberg, Elinor Glyn, Robert Graves, Kerry Greenwood, Elly Griffiths, Thomas Hardy, Jane Harper, Hermann Hesse, Patricia Highsmith, Elizabeth Jane Howard, Bohumil Hrabal, Victor Hugo, Aldous Huxley, Thomas Huxley, Marlon James, P.D. James, Tove Jansson, Gertrude Jekyll, Michael Joseph, Jack Kerouac, Judith Kerr, Stephen King, Satoshi Kitamura, Ursula Le Guin, John Lennon, Cecil Day Lewis, Anat Levit, Pierre Loti, H.P. Lovecraft, Compton Mackenzie, Olivia Manning, Ngaio Marsh, W.S. Maugham, Alberto Moravia, Jan Morris, Harold Munro, Haruki Murakami, Iris Murdoch, V.S. Naipaul, Irène Némirovsky, Helen Nicoll, Audrey Niffenegger, Anaïs Nin, Sven Nordqvist, Joyce Carol Oates, Jirō Osaragi, Sylvia Plath, Edgar Allan Poe, Beatrix Potter, Ezra Pound, Anthony Powell, Terry Pratchett, Barbara Pym, Ayn Rand, Rainer Maria Rilke, Christina Rossetti, Françoise Sagan, Saki, J.D. Salinger, C.J. Sansom, Jean-Paul Sartre, Albert Schweitzer, Walter Scott, George Bernard Shaw, Preeti Shenoy, Edith Sitwell, John Skelton, Alexander McCall Smith, Edith Södergran, Pajtim Statovci, Gloria Steinem, Mary Stewart, Harriet Beecher Stowe, Algernon Charles Swinburne, Hunter S.

Thompson, Jules Verne, Gore Vidal, Alice Walker, Sylvia Townsend Warner, H.G. Wells, Patrick White, Tennessee Williams, William Carlos Williams, P.G. Wodehouse, Cecil Woodham-Smith, Virginia Woolf, William Wordsworth, Bing Xin, W.B. Yeats and Émile Zola. No matter the nationality, whether urban or rural, old or young, poor or rich, writers throughout history have turned to cats.

'All poets love cats',[3] Dame Edith Sitwell once stated. Fortunately, not only poets, but novelists, playwrights, essayists and historians have become willing slaves to cats. Those miraculously soft, sheathed paws have made their mark on fiction. In the studies of writers, cats have been silent, and sometimes helpful, witnesses to the creation of masterpieces. It is to be hoped that, as long as fingers wield a pen, or tap away at the keys of a computer, somewhere nearby a cat, curled up on a desk or sofa, will be purring contentedly, knowing that its paws behind the pen have forever enriched our literary world.

THE END

# NOTES

INTRODUCTION

1. James Herriot, *James Herriot's Cat Stories*, Bantam Books, London, 1994, p. 10.
2. T.S. Eliot, *The Complete Poems and Plays*, Faber & Faber, London, 1969, p. 209.
3. Charles Dickens, *David Copperfield*, Flame Tree Publishing, London, 2019, p. 677.
4. Aldous Huxley, *Music at Night and Other Essays*, Country Life Press, Garden City NY, 1931, p. 230.
5. Michel de Montaigne, *The Complete Essays of Montaigne*, trans. Donald M. Frame, Stanford University Press, Stanford CA, 1957, p. 331.

DR JOHNSON

1. Robert Browning, *The Pied Piper of Hamelin*, Frederick Warne, London, 1903, p. 6.
2. Samuel Johnson, *Johnson's Dictionary: A Modern Selection*, Pantheon, New York, 1963, p. 114.
3. James Boswell, *Boswell's Life of Johnson*, vol. II, Everyman, London, 1960, p. 452.
4. Ibid.
5. Henry Hitchings, *The World in Thirty-Eight Chapters or Dr Johnson's Guide to Life*, Macmillan, London, 2018, p. 173.
6. Percival Stockdale, *The Memoirs of the Life, and Writings of Percival Stockdale: Containing Many Interesting Anecdotes of the Illustrious Men with Whom He Was Connected*, vol. I, Longman, Hurst, Rees & Orme, London, 1809, p. 79.

7. Percival Stockdale, 'An Elegy on the Death of Dr Johnson's Favourite Cat', *Universal Magazine*, May 1771.
8. Samuel Johnson, *The Letters of Samuel Johnson*, ed. Bruce Redford, Princeton University Press, Princeton NJ, 1994, p. 241.
9. Boswell, *Boswell's Life of Johnson*, vol. II, p. 452.
10. Leigh Hunt, *Essays by Leigh Hunt*, ed. Arthur Symons, Walter Scott, London, 1887, p. 268.

HORACE WALPOLE

1. Christopher Frayling, *Horace Walpole's Cat*, Thames & Hudson, London, 2009, p. 13.
2. A 'tabby' is not a breed of cat, but is rather a coat type, common in domestic felines. Tabby is a pattern that occurs naturally and is characterized by stripes and flecked and banded patterns in the fur. In Walpole's day, the word 'tabby' more commonly denoted a striped silk taffeta (from the French word *tabis*). The term 'tabby cat' was first used in England in the 1690s, and by Walpole's day had been shortened to simply 'tabby', while the fabric meaning was starting to disappear from common use.
3. Frayling, *Horace Walpole's Cat*, p. 17.
4. Ibid., p. 24.
5. Ibid., pp. 59–64.
6. Ibid., p. 40.
7. Ibid., p. 67.
8. Christopher Smart, *My Cat Jeoffry: A Poem*, Pelican Books, London, 1992, pp. 9–12.
9. 'Rejoice in the Lamb, Op. 30-2, For I will Consider my Cat Jeoffry', www.youtube.com/watch?v=iZ_sinj5lOc.

ROBERT SOUTHEY

1. Robert Southey, *The Doctor, &c.*, Longman, Brown, Green & Longmans, London, 1847, p. 593. Chrysolite is a yellowish-green gemstone, a brownish variety of olivine.
2. C.C. Southey, *The Life and Correspondence of Robert Southey*, Longman, Brown, Green & Longman's, London, 1850, p. 191.
3. Southey, *The Doctor, &c.*, p. 328.
4. Ibid., p. 683.
5. Southey, *The Life and Correspondence of Robert Southey*, p. 210.
6. Southey, *The Doctor, &c.*, p. 585.
7. Ibid., p. 386.
8. Ibid., p. 587.

9. Ibid., p. 588.
10. Ibid., p. 582.
11. Ibid., p. 588.
12. Ibid., p. 684.
13. Ibid., pp. 589–90.
14. Ibid., p. 685.
15. Ibid., p. 592.
16. Edward Dowden, *Southey*, ed. John Morley, Harper & Bros, New York, 1887, p. 96.
17. Southey, *The Doctor, &c.*, p. 685.
18. Robert Southey, *Letters of Robert Southey: A Selection*, ed. Maurice H. Fitzgerald, Oxford University Press, London, 1912, p. 391.
19. Southey, *The Life and Correspondence of Robert Southey*, p. 223.
20. Ibid., pp. 210–11.
21. Southey, *The Doctor, &c.*, p. 682.
22. Hartley Coleridge, *Poems by Hartley Coleridge: With a Memoir of His Life by his Brother*, Moxon, London, 1851, p. 253.
23. William Guthrie, *The Life and Adventures of a Cat*, Willoughby Mynors, London, 1760, p. 14.

ALEXANDRE DUMAS

1. Alexandre Dumas, *My Pets*, trans. Alfred Allinson, Macmillan, New York, 1909, pp. 89–90.
2. France passed its first animal protection law in 1850, although this law only prohibited public cruelty towards animals. In 1976 France became one of the first countries in the world to officially recognize animal sentience.
3. Katharine M. Rogers, *Cat*, Reaktion Books, London, 2006, p. 123.
4. Anatole France, *The Crime of Sylvestre Bonnard*, E.A. Petherick, London, 1891, p. 3.
5. Charles Baudelaire, *Intimate Journals*, trans. Christopher Isherwood, Methuen, London, 1949, p. 16.
6. John M.F. Wright, *Alma Mater; or, Seven Years at the University of Cambridge. By a Trinity Man*, vol. I, Black, Young, & Young, London, 1827, p. 17.
7. Geoffrey Chaucer, *The Canterbury Tales*, J.M. Dent, London, 1968, p. 92.

EDWARD LEAR

1. Jenny Uglow, *Mr Lear: A Life of Art and Nonsense*, Faber & Faber, London, 2017, p. 291.

2. Peter Levi, *Edward Lear: A Life*, Tauris Parke, London, 1995, p. 258.
3. Uglow, *Mr Lear*, p. 118.
4. Levi, *Edward Lear: A Life*, p. 320.
5. Vivien Noakes, *Edward Lear: The Life of a Wanderer*, Sutton Publishing, Stroud, 1968, p. 223.
6. Levi, *Edward Lear: A Life*, p. 288.
7. Edward Lear, *Later Letters of Edward Lear*, ed. Lady Strachey, T. Fisher Unwin, London, 1911, p. 301.
8. Levi, *Edward Lear: A Life*, p. 295.
9. The Pirouet Alphabet is now in London's Victoria and Albert Museum, but was reproduced in 1953; the 'C for Cat' illustration often appears on greetings cards.
10. Edward Lear, *The Complete Verse and Other Nonsense*, ed. Vivien Noakes, Penguin Books, London, 2001, p. 428.
11. Ibid., p. 541.
12. Ibid., p. 353.
13. Levi, *Edward Lear: A Life*, p. 302.
14. Ibid., p. 266.
15. Edward Lear, *Selected Letters*, ed. Vivien Noakes, Oxford University Press, Oxford, 1990, p. 275.
16. Levi, *Edward Lear: A Life*, p. 290.
17. Uglow, *Mr Lear*, p. 516.
18. Lear, *Selected Letters*, p. 282.
19. Ibid., p. 282.
20. 'Foss (cat)', Wikipedia, https://en.wikipedia.org/wiki/Foss_(cat).
21. 'The Cat', *Sydney Morning Herald*, 31 July 1857.

CHARLES DICKENS

1. This wonderful collection was made possible by the eager book-collecting and generosity of two brothers. It was established at the library in 1940.
2. Charles Dickens, *Our Mutual Friend*, Penguin, London, 1997, p. 91.
3. Charles Dickens, *Bleak House*, Collector's Library, London, 2006, p. 213.
4. Charles Dickens, *The Uncommercial Traveller*, ed. Daniel Tyler, Oxford University Press, Oxford, 2015, p. 103.
5. Mamie Dickens, *My Father as I Recall Him*, Roxburghe Press, London, 1897, pp. 81–2.
6. Mamie Dickens, *My Father as I Recall Him*, p. 82.

7. Francis Grose, *A Classical Dictionary of the Vulgar Tongue*, S. Hooper, London, 1788, p. 104.
8. Lewis Carroll, *The Complete Illustrated Works of Lewis Carroll*, Chancellor Press, London, 1982, p. 65.

MARK TWAIN

1. Clara Clemens, *My Father, Mark Twain*, Harper & Brothers, New York, 1931, p. 257.
2. Ibid., p. 257.
3. *Kansas City Star*, 5 April 1905.
4. Mark Dawidziak, *Mark Twain for Cat Lovers*, Rowman & Littlefield, Lanham MD, 2016, p. 115.
5. *The Wit and Wisdom of Mark Twain*, compiled by Jennifer Boudinot, Chartwell Books, New York, 2016, p. 135.
6. Mark Twain, *Mark Twain's Notebook*, ed. Alfred Bigelow Paine, Harper Brothers, New York, 1935, pp. 236–7.
7. Mark Twain, *Pudd'nhead Wilson*, Penguin Books, Harmondsworth, 1969, p. 56.
8. *San Francisco Chronicle*, 2 October 2008.
9. Alison Nastasi, *Writers and Their Cats*, Chronicle Books, San Francisco CA, 2018, p. 76.
10. Mark Twain, *Autobiography of Mark Twain*, vol. I, ed. Benjamin Griffin and Harriet Elinor Smith, University of California Press, Berkeley CA, 2010, p. 345.
11. Dawidziak, *Mark Twain for Cat Lovers*, p. 75.
12. Nastasi, *Writers and Their Cats*, p. 76.
13. Mark Twain, *Autobiography of Mark Twain*, vol. II, ed. Benjamin Griffin and Harriet Elinor Smith, University of California Press, Berkeley CA, 2013, p. 248.
14. Ibid., p. 216.
15. Mark Twain, *Mark Twain's Letters*, ed. Albert Bigelow Paine, Harper & Brothers, New York, 1929, p. 821.
16. Nastasi, *Writers and Their Cats*, p. 76.
17. Twain, *Autobiography of Mark Twain*, vol. II, p. 248.
18. Mark Twain, *The Adventures of Tom Sawyer*, Viking, New York, 1995, p. 108.
19. Ibid., pp. 107–8.
20. Mark Twain, *Mark Twain's Fables of Man*, ed. John S. Tuckey, University of California Press, Berkeley CA, 1972, p. 180.
21. Mark Twain, *No. 44, The Mysterious Stranger*, University of California Press, Berkeley CA, 1969, p. 18.

22. Mark Twain, *Collected Non Fiction*, vol. 2, Everyman's Library, New York, 2016, p. 374.
23. Mark Twain, *Rambling Notes of an Idle Excursion*, Rose–Belford Publishing, Toronto, 1878, p. 43.
24. Mark Twain, *Following the Equator*, Dover, New York, 1989, p. 256.
25. Twain, *Mark Twain's Notebook*, pp. 236–7.

COLETTE

1. Judith Thurman, *Secrets of the Flesh: A Life of Colette*, Alfred A. Knopf, New York, 1999, p. 23.
2. Colette's birthplace is today privately owned, but the owners have two cats who roam the garden, which looks much as it did in Colette's childhood.
3. Thurman, *Secrets of the Flesh*, p. 104.
4. The exact role Willy played in the Claudine novels is still being debated, but today they appear under Colette's name, not his.
5. Colette, *Claudine in Paris*, Vintage, London, 1958, p. 38.
6. Alison Nastasi, *Writers and Their Cats*, Chronicle Books, San Francisco CA, 2018, p. 35.
7. Colette, *Gigi, and The Cat*, Penguin Books, Harmondsworth, 1944, p. 79.
8. Thurman, *Secrets of the Flesh*, p. 398.
9. Colette, *Gigi, and The Cat*, p. 71.
10. Thurman, *Secrets of the Flesh*, p. 397.
11. Ibid., p. 398.
12. Judith Robinson and Scott Pack, *Literary Cats*, Bodleian Library Publishing, Oxford, 2022, p. 122.

L.M. MONTGOMERY

1. Francis W.P. Bolger, *The Years Before Anne: The Early Career of Lucy Maud Montgomery, Author of Anne of Green Gables*, Nimbus Publishing, Halifax NS, 1991, p. 189.
2. E. Weber, 'L.M. Montgomery as a Letter Writer', *Dalhousie Review*, vol. 22, no. 3, 1942, p. 309.
3. *The Lucy Maud Montgomery Album*, compiled by Kevin McCabe, ed. Alexandra Heilbron, Fitzhenry & Whiteside, Toronto ON, 1999, p. 142.
4. Ibid., p. 140.
5. L.M. Montgomery, *The Complete Journals of L.M. Montgomery: The PEI Years, 1901–1911*, ed. Mary Henley Rubio and Elizabeth Hillman Waterston, Oxford University Press, Don Mills ON, 1985, p. 120.

6. *The Lucy Maud Montgomery Album*, p. 142.
7. Montgomery, *The Complete Journals of L.M. Montgomery: The PEI Years*, p. 264.
8. Ibid.
9. *The Lucy Maud Montgomery Album*, p. 139.
10. Montgomery, *The Complete Journals of L.M. Montgomery: The PEI Years*, p. 265.
11. Ibid.
12. *The Lucy Maud Montgomery Album*, p. 137.
13. Montgomery, *The Complete Journals of L.M. Montgomery: The PEI Years*, p. 265.
14. Ibid., p. 370.
15. Ibid., p. 371.
16. Ibid., p. 395.
17. Maud's husband's name was actually Ewen, but she always spelled his name Ewan.
18. Montgomery, *The Complete Journals of L.M. Montgomery: The PEI Years*, p. 420.
19. Ibid., p. 395.
20. *The Lucy Maud Montgomery Album*, p. 143.
21. Montgomery, *The Complete Journals of L.M. Montgomery: The PEI Years*, p. 265.
22. Mary Henley Rubio, *Lucy Maud Montgomery: The Gift of Wings*, Anchor Canada, Toronto ON, 2008, p. 498.
23. *The Lucy Maud Montgomery Album*, p. 143.
24. L.M. Montgomery, *The Selected Journals of L.M. Montgomery*, Volume IV: *1925–1935*, ed. Mary Henley Rubio and Elizabeth Waterston, Oxford University Press, Toronto ON, 1988, p. 358.
25. L.M. Montgomery, *The Selected Journals of L.M. Montgomery*, Volume V: *1935–1942*, ed. Mary Henley Rubio and Elizabeth Waterston, Oxford University Press, Toronto ON, 2004, p. 124.
26. L.M. Montgomery, *Jane of Lantern Hill*, Angus & Robertson, Sydney, 1937, p. 1.
27. Rubio, *Lucy Maud Montgomery: The Gift of Wings*, p. 498.
28. Montgomery, *The Selected Journals of L.M. Montgomery*, vol. V, p. 142.
29. Rubio, *Lucy Maud Montgomery: The Gift of Wings*, p. 499.
30. *The Lucy Maud Montgomery Album*, p. 143.
31. L.M. Montgomery, *The Blue Castle*, Angus & Robertson, Sydney, 1937, p. 91.

32. L.M. Montgomery, *Anne of the Island*, L.C. Page, Boston MA, 1966, p. 112.
33. Ibid., pp. 194–5.
34. Ibid., p. 219.
35. L.M. Montgomery, *Rilla of Ingleside*, Angus & Robertson, Sydney, 1937, p. 4.
36. L.M. Montgomery, *Emily of New Moon*, Harrap, London, 1977, p. 41.
37. L.M. Montgomery, *The Story Girl*, Angus & Robertson, Sydney, 1976, p. 13.
38. Montgomery, *The Complete Journals of L.M. Montgomery: The PEI Years*, p. 404.
39. Montgomery, *The Story Girl*, p. 14.
40. Weber, 'L.M. Montgomery as a Letter Writer', p. 309.
41. Rudyard Kipling, *Just So Stories*, Macmillan, London, 1953, p. 206.

## WINSTON CHURCHILL

1. William Manchester, *The Last Lion: Winston Spencer Churchill, Visions of Glory, 1874–1932*, Bantam, London, 1984, p. 778.
2. Anthony Eden, *The Reckoning*, Houghton Mifflin, Boston MA, 1965, p. 339.
3. Mary Soames (ed.), *Winston and Clementine: The Personal Letters of the Churchills*, Houghton Mifflin, Boston MA, 1999, p. 471.
4. James Humes, *The Wit and Wisdom of Winston Churchill*, HarperCollins, New York, 2007, p. 204.
5. David Dilks, *Churchill and Company*, Bloomsbury, London, 2012, p. 44.
6. The voluntary National Air Raid Precautions for Animals Committee could issue a NARPAC collar and recognition disc to pets that read 'Finder Please Report this Number to Nearest National Animal Guard', so that pets could be reunited with owners if found straying when bombs fell, but it was more usually dogs that wore such collars. Most cats were left lost and terrified.
7. Martin Gilbert and Larry P. Arnn (eds), *The Churchill Documents*, Volume XVIII: *One Continent*, Hillsdale College Press, Hillsdale MI, 2015, pp. 433–4.

## ERNEST HEMINGWAY

1. Ernest Hemingway, *Islands in the Stream*, Bantam Books, New York, 1972, p. 198.
2. Carlos Baker, *Ernest Hemingway: A Life Story*, Bantam Books, New York, 1969, p. 491.

3. Alison Nastasi, *Writers and Their Cats*, Chronicle Books, San Francisco CA, 2018, p. 44.
4. Carlene Fredericka Brennen, *Hemingway's Cats*, Pineapple Press, Sarasota FL, 2006, p. 71.
5. Hemingway, *Islands in the Stream*, p. 227.
6. Nastasi, *Writers and Their Cats*, p. 44.
7. Hemingway, *Islands in the Stream*, p. 205.
8. Mary Welsh Hemingway, *How It Was*, Alfred A. Knopf, New York, 1951, p. 175.
9. Ernest Hemingway, *A Moveable Feast*, Arrow Books, London, 2011, p. 113.
10. Ernest Hemingway, *Ernest Hemingway: Selected Letters, 1917–1961*, ed. Carlos Baker, Charles Scribner's Sons, New York, 1982, p. 555.
11. President Teddy Roosevelt had a polydactyl cat named Slippers.
12. Brennen, *Hemingway's Cats*, p. 31.
13. Hemingway, *Ernest Hemingway: Selected Letters*, p. 555.
14. Leicester Hemingway, *My Brother, Ernest Hemingway*, Pineapple Press, Sarasota FL, 1996, p. 278.
15. Fernand Méry, *The Life, History and Magic of the Cat*, trans. Emma Street, Paul Hamlyn, London, 1967, p. 219.
16. Alison Nastasi, *Writers and Their Cats*, Chronicle Books, San Francisco CA, 2018, p. 44.
17. Hemingway, *Islands in the Stream*, p. 200.
18. Hemingway, *Ernest Hemingway: Selected Letters*, p. 858.
19. Mary Welsh Hemingway, *How It Was*, p. 502.

MARGARET MITCHELL

1. Margaret Mitchell, *Gone with the Wind*, Macmillan, New York, 1936.
2. Darden Asbury Pyron, *Southern Daughter: The Life of Margaret Mitchell*, Oxford University Press, Oxford, 1991, p. 28.
3. Marianne Walker, *Margaret Mitchell and John Marsh: A Biography*, Peachtree Publishing, Atlanta GA, 1993, p. 355.
4. Ibid., p. 356.
5. Ibid.
6. Walker, *Margaret Mitchell and John Marsh*, p. 356.
7. Ibid., p. 495.
8. Robert Edward Lee, *The Recollections and Letters of General Robert E. Lee*, William S. Konecky Associates, New York, 1998, p. 248.
9. Mitchell, *Gone with the Wind*, p. 3.
10. Ibid., p. 475.
11. Ibid., p. 641.

12. Ibid., p. 838.
13. *The Illustrated London News*, 13 March 1948.
14. *The Stage*, 14 January 1956.

DOROTHY L. SAYERS

1. Dorothy L. Sayers, *Have His Carcase*, New English Library, London, 1974, p. 127.
2. Dorothy L. Sayers, *The Letters of Dorothy L. Sayers, 1899–1936*, Volume 1: *The Making of a Detective Novelist*, ed. Barbara Reynolds, Hodder & Stoughton, London, 1995, pp. 192–3. Lord Peter Wimsey was the gentleman detective who featured in the books Sayers was now writing. Hero of eleven novels and various short stories (all classics of the detective genre), Lord Peter is frequently described as 'cat-like'.
3. I Samuel 15:32.
4. Sayers, *The Letters of Dorothy L. Sayers, 1899–1936*, vol. 1, p. 257.
5. Ibid., pp. 258–9.
6. Ibid., p. 282.
7. Ibid., p. 301.
8. Ibid., p. 324.
9. Ibid., p. 335.
10. Ibid., p. 331.
11. Dorothy L. Sayers, *The Letters of Dorothy L. Sayers, 1944–1950*, Volume 3: *A Noble Daring*, ed. Barbara Reynolds, Dorothy L. Sayers Society, Witham, 1998, p. 326.
12. Dorothy L. Sayers, *Poetry of Dorothy L. Sayers*, ed. Ralph E. Hone, Dorothy L. Sayers Society, Witham, in association with the Marion E. Wade Center, Wheaton IL, 1996, p. 136.
13. A huge 80 per cent of ginger cats are male – the 'ginger gene' which produces the orange colour is on the X chromosome.
14. Mo Moulton, *Mutual Admiration Society: How Dorothy L. Sayers and Her Oxford Circle Remade the World for Women*, Corsair, London, 2019, p. 276.
15. Sayers, *The Letters of Dorothy L. Sayers, 1944–1950*, p. 325.
16. Ibid., p. 346.
17. Ibid.
18. Dorothy L. Sayers, *The Letters of Dorothy L. Sayers, 1951–1957*, Volume 4: *In the Midst of Life*, ed. Barbara Reynolds, Dorothy L. Sayers Society, Witham, 2000, p. 99.
19. Ibid.
20. John Doubleday, email to Susannah Fullerton, 29 November 2022.

21. Janet Hitchman, *Such a Strange Lady: A Biography of Dorothy L. Sayers*, New English Library, London, 1975, p. 191.
22. Torquato Tasso was a sixteenth-century Italian poet.
23. Sayers, *The Letters of Dorothy L. Sayers, 1944–1950*, p. 512.
24. Moulton, *Mutual Admiration Society*, p. 278.
25. Sayers, *The Letters of Dorothy L. Sayers, 1951–1957*, p. 120.
26. Ibid., p. 55.
27. Ibid., p. 124.
28. Ibid., p. 122.
29. Ibid., p. 94.
30. Sayers, *The Letters of Dorothy L. Sayers, 1899–1936*, p. 251.
31. Sayers, *The Letters of Dorothy L. Sayers, 1951–1957*, p. 251.
32. Ibid., p. 238.
33. Ibid., p. 280.
34. Ibid., p. 406.
35. Dorothy L. Sayers, *Busman's Honeymoon*, Hodder & Stoughton, London, 2016, p. 81.
36. Dorothy L. Sayers, *Gaudy Night*, Hodder & Stoughton, London, 2003, p. xii.
37. Heraldic names for cats include 'cat-a-mount', 'catamount' and 'musion'.
38. Moulton, *Mutual Admiration Society*, p. 278.
39. Sayers, *The Letters of Dorothy L. Sayers, 1951–1957*, p. 55.
40. Ibid., p. 124.
41. Eliot won the Nobel Prize for Literature in 1948, after the publication of his cat poems.
42. T.S. Eliot, *The Complete Poems and Plays*, Faber & Faber, London, 1969, p. 235.

PAUL GALLICO

1. Jerome Holtzman, 'The Gallico Adventure', *New York Magazine*, vol. 7, no. 18, 1974, p. 34.
2. Paul Gallico, *The Silent Miaow*, Crown, New York, 1964, p. 114.
3. Paul Gallico, *Honorable Cat*, Greenwich House, New York, 1971, p. 1.
4. Paul Gallico, *Jennie*, Penguin, Harmondsworth, 1963, p. 12.
5. Gallico, *The Silent Miaow*, p. 11.
6. Ibid., p. 67.
7. Ibid., p. 110.
8. Ibid., p. 156.
9. Ibid., p. 158.
10. Ibid.

11. Paul Gallico, *Honorable Cat*, Crown, New York, 1972, Dedication.
12. Kitty Litter was invented in 1947 by American Edward Lowe.
13. Gallico, *Honorable Cat*, p. 26.
14. Gallico, *The Silent Miaow*, p. 97.
15. Gallico, *Honorable Cat*, p. 112.
16. Ibid., p. 44.
17. *The Collins Book of Nursery Rhymes*, HarperCollins, London, 1990, p. 26.

MURIEL SPARK

1. Martin Stannard, *Muriel Spark: The Biography*, W.W. Norton, New York, 2010, p. 199.
2. Ibid., p. 17.
3. Muriel Spark, *The Informed Air: Essays*, ed. Penelope Jardine, New Directions, New York, 2014, p. 277.
4. Ibid., p. 277.
5. Ibid., p. 275.
6. Alan Taylor, *Appointment in Arezzo: A Friendship with Muriel Spark*, Polygon, Edinburgh, 2017, p. 39.
7. Stannard, *Muriel Spark: The Biography*, p. 129.
8. Spark, *The Informed Air: Essays*, p. 278.
9. Ibid., pp. 277–8.
10. Muriel Spark, *A Far Cry from Kensington*, Houghton Mifflin, Boston MA, 1988, pp. 93–4.
11. Spark, *The Informed Air: Essays*, p. 277.
12. Ibid., p. 275.
13. Stannard, *Muriel Spark: The Biography*, p. 199.
14. Muriel Spark, *All the Poems of Muriel Spark*, ed. Penelope Jardine, New Directions, New York, 2004, p. 78.
15. Spark, *The Informed Air: Essays*, p. 277.
16. Muriel Spark, *Robinson*, New Directions, New York, 1958, p. 11.
17. Ibid., p. 41.
18. Ibid., p. 42.
19. Ibid., p. 43.
20. Stannard, *Muriel Spark: The Biography*, p. 199.
21. Spark, *The Informed Air: Essays*, p. 278.
22. Ibid.
23. Judith Robinson and Scott Pack, *Literary Cats*, Bodleian Library Publishing, Oxford, 2022, pp. 130–31.
24. Spark, *The Informed Air: Essays*, p. 277.

### DORIS LESSING

1. Carole Klein, *Doris Lessing: A Biography*, Duckworth, London, 2000, p. 155.
2. Doris Lessing, *Particularly Cats and More Cats*, Michael Joseph, London, 1967, p. 3.
3. Ibid., p. 10.
4. Ibid., p. 12.
5. Ibid., p. 13.
6. Doris experimented with many names for this cat – Melissa, Franny, Suzette, Marilyn, Sappho and Circe – but in the end 'Grey Cat' was what stuck.
7. Lessing, *Particularly Cats and More Cats*, p. 55.
8. Ibid., p. 57.
9. Ibid., p. 125.
10. Ibid., p. 137.
11. Doris Lessing, *The Old Age of El Magnifico*, Flamingo, London, 2000, p. 3.
12. Ibid., p. 9.
13. Alison Nastasi, *Writers and Their Cats*, Chronicle Books, San Francisco CA, 2018, p. 36.
14. Ibid., p. 36.
15. Lessing, *The Old Age of El Magnifico*, p. 10.
16. Ibid., p. 11.
17. Lessing, *Particularly Cats and More Cats*, p. 48.
18. Ibid., p. 138.
19. Lessing, *The Old Age of El Magnifico*, p. 16.
20. Ibid., p. 21.
21. Ibid., p. 32.
22. Klein, *Doris Lessing: A Biography*, p. 246.
23. Ibid., p. 247.

### LYNLEY DODD

1. Lynley Dodd, *Hairy Maclary from Donaldson's Dairy*, Penguin Books New Zealand, Auckland, 2014, p. 29.
2. I'd have loved to include Jane Austen in this book, but there's simply not enough material. Jane Austen refers in a letter to playing with a black kitten in a Bath lodging house, but otherwise felines are sadly absent from her works.
3. Jane Austen, *Jane Austen's Letters*, ed. Deirdre le Faye, Oxford University Press, Oxford, 1995, p. 20.

4. Lynley Dodd, *Furry Tales: A Treasury of Cat Mischief*, Penguin Books New Zealand, Auckland, 2018, p. 7.
5. Dodd, *Hairy Maclary from Donaldson's Dairy*, p. 27.
6. Dodd, *Furry Tales*, p. 7.
7. Finlay Macdonald, *The Life and Art of Lynley Dodd*, Penguin Books New Zealand, Auckland, 2013, p. 81.
8. Dodd, *Furry Tales*, p. 8.
9. Macdonald, *The Life and Art of Lynley Dodd*, p. 80.
10. For example, Wooskit appears as the doctor's cat in *The Minister's Cat ABC*, Penguin Books New Zealand, Auckland, 1994.
11. Dodd, *Furry Tales*, p. 8.
12. Ibid., p. 13.
13. Ibid., p. 23.
14. Ibid., p. 39.
15. Aung San Suu Kyi, who shares Lynley's love of Jane Austen, was once given a Burmese cat by a man concerned that Myanmar (formerly Burma) had very few Burmese cats, but her dog took an instant dislike to the cat and it had to be returned to the donor.
16. Dodd, *Furry Tales*, p. 9.
17. Lynley Dodd, email to Susannah Fullerton, 23 February 2003.
18. Dodd, *Furry Tales*, p. 17.

TAILPIECE

1. Théophile Gautier, *Charles Baudelaire: His Life*, Brentano's, New York, 1915, p. 41.
2. Charles Baudelaire, *Selected Poems*, Penguin Books, Harmondsworth, 1975, p. 127.
3. Honor Clerk, *The Sitwells and the Arts of the 1920s and 1930s*, University of Texas Press, Austin TX, 1996, p. 157.

# FURTHER READING

### DR JOHNSON

Boswell, James, *Boswell's Life of Johnson*, Everyman, London, 1960.
Hibbert, Christopher, *The Personal History of Samuel Johnson*, Penguin Books, Harmondsworth, 1984.
Hitchings, Henry, *The World in Thirty-Eight Chapters or Dr Johnson's Guide to Life*, Macmillan, London, 2018.
Martin, Peter, *Samuel Johnson: A Biography*, Weidenfeld & Nicolson, London, 2008.
Stockdale, Percival, 'An Elegy on the Death of Dr Johnson's Favourite Cat', *Universal Magazine*, May 1771.

### HORACE WALPOLE

Frayling, Christopher, *Horace Walpole's Cat*, Thames & Hudson, London, 2009.

### ROBERT SOUTHEY

Coleridge, Hartley, *Poems by Hartley Coleridge: With a Memoir of His Life by his Brother*, Moxon, London, 1851.
Dowden, Edward, *Southey*, ed. John Morley, Harper & Bros, New York, 1887, p. 96.
Southey, Robert, *The Doctor, &c.*, Longman, Brown, Green & Longman's, London, 1847.
Southey, Robert, *The Life and Correspondence of Robert Southey*, ed. Charles Southey, Longman, Brown, Green & Longman's, London, 1849.
Storey, Mark, *Robert Southey: A Life*, Oxford University Press, Oxford, 1997.

## ALEXANDRE DUMAS

Dumas, Alexandre, *My Pets*, trans. Alfred Allinson, Macmillan, New York, 1909.
France, Anatole, *The Crime of Sylvestre Bonnard*, E.A. Petherick, London, 1891.

## EDWARD LEAR

Kamen, Gloria, *Edward Lear, King of Nonsense: A Biography*, Simon & Schuster, New York, 1990.
Lear, Edward, *Edward Lear: Selected Letters*, Clarendon Press, Oxford, 1988.
Lear, Edward, *The Complete Verse and Other Nonsense*, ed. Vivien Noakes, Penguin Books, London, 2001.
Levi, Peter, *Edward Lear: A Life*, Tauris Parke Publisher, London, 1995.
Noakes, Vivien, *Edward Lear: The Life of a Wanderer*, Sutton, Stroud, 2004.
Uglow, Jenny, *Mr Lear: A Life of Art and Nonsense*, Faber & Faber, London, 2017.

## CHARLES DICKENS

Ackroyd, Peter, *Dickens*, Minerva, London, 1990.
Dickens, Charles, *Our Mutual Friend*, Penguin, London, 1997.
Dickens, Charles, *Bleak House*, Collector's Library, London, 2006.
Dickens, Charles, *The Uncommercial Traveller*, ed. Daniel Tyler, Oxford University Press, Oxford, 2015.
Tomalin, Claire, *Charles Dickens: A Life*, Viking, London, 2011.

## MARK TWAIN

Clemens, Clara, *My Father, Mark Twain*, Harper & Brothers, New York, 1931.
Dawidziak, Mark, *Mark Twain for Cat Lovers*, Rowman & Littlefield, Lanham MD, 2016.
Maltbie, P.I., *Bambino and Mr Twain*, Penguin, New York, 2019.
Twain, Mark, *Autobiography of Mark Twain*, ed. Benjamin Griffin and Harriet Elinor Smith, University of California Press, Berkeley CA, 2010.
Twain, Mark, *Rambling Notes of an Idle Excursion*, Rose-Belford Publishing, Toronto, 1878.
Twain, Mark, *Mark Twain's Letters*, ed. Albert Bigelow Paine, Harper & Bros, New York, 1929.
Twain, Mark, *Mark Twain's Notebook*, ed. Alfred Bigelow Paine, Harper & Brothers, New York, 1935.

Twain, Mark, *Pudd'nhead Wilson*, Penguin Books, London, 1969.
Twain, Mark, *Following the Equator*, Dover, New York, 1989.
Twain, Mark, *The Adventures of Tom Sawyer*, Viking, New York, 1995.

### L.M. MONTGOMERY

McCabe, Kevin, *The Lucy Maud Montgomery Album*, Fitzhenry & Whiteside, Toronto, 1999.
Montgomery, L.M., *Jane of Lantern Hill*, Angus & Robertson, Sydney, 1937.
Montgomery, L.M., *The Blue Castle*, Angus & Robertson, Sydney, 1937.
Montgomery, L.M., *Rilla of Ingleside*, Angus & Robertson, Sydney, 1937.
Montgomery, L.M., *Anne of the Island*, L.C. Page, Boston MA, 1966.
Montgomery, L.M., *The Story Girl*, Angus & Robertson, Sydney, 1976.
Montgomery, L.M., *Emily of New Moon*, Harrap, London, 1977.
Montgomery, L.M., *The Complete Journals of L.M. Montgomery, The PEI Years, 1901–1911*, ed. Mary Henley Rubio and Elizabeth Hillman Waterston, Oxford University Press, Toronto ON, 1985.
Rubio, Mary Henley, *Lucy Maud Montgomery: The Gift of Wings*, Anchor Canada, Toronto ON, 2008.

### WINSTON CHURCHILL

Dilks, David, *Churchill and Company*, Bloomsbury, London, 2012.
Eden, Anthony, *The Reckoning*, Houghton Mifflin, Boston MA, 1965.
Lovell, Mary S., *The Churchills: A Family at the Heart of History from the Duke of Marlborough to Winston Churchill*, W.W. Norton, New York, 2011.
Manchester, William, *The Last Lion: Winston Spencer Churchill, Visions of Glory, 1874–1932*, Bantam Books, London, 1984.
Soames, Mary (ed.), *Winston and Clementine: The Personal Letters of the Churchills*, Houghton Mifflin, Boston MA, 1999.
Trethewey, Rachel, *The Churchill Girls: The Story of Winston's Daughters*, History Press, Cheltenham, 2021.

### ERNEST HEMINGWAY

Baker, Carlos, *Ernest Hemingway: A Life Story*, Bantam Books, New York, 1969.
Brennen, Carlene Fredericka, *Hemingway's Cats*, Pineapple Press, Sarasota FL, 2006.
Hemingway, Ernest, *A Moveable Feast*, Arrow Books, London, 2011.
Hemingway, Ernest, *Ernest Hemingway: Selected Letters*, ed. Carlos Baker, Charles Scribner's Sons, New York, 1982.
Hemingway, Ernest, *Islands in the Stream*, Bantam Books, New York, 1972.

Hemingway, Mary Welsh, *How It Was*, Alfred A. Knopf, New York, 1951.

## MARGARET MITCHELL

Edwards, Anne, *Road to Tara: The Life of Margaret Mitchell*, Dell, New York, 1983.
Mitchell, Margaret, *Gone with the Wind*, Warner Books, New York, 1999.
Pyron, Darden Asbury, *Southern Daughter: The Life of Margaret Mitchell*, Oxford University Press, Oxford, 1991.
Walker, Marianne, *Margaret Mitchell and John Marsh: The Love Story Behind Gone with the Wind*, Peachtree Publishers, Atlanta GA, 1993.

## DOROTHY L. SAYERS

Brabazon, James, *Dorothy L. Sayers: A Biography*, Victor Gollancz, London, 1988.
Hitchman, Janet, *Such a Strange Lady: A Biography of Dorothy L. Sayers*, New English Library, London, 1975.
Moulton, Mo, *The Mutual Admiration Society: How Dorothy L. Sayers and Her Oxford Circle Remade the World for Women*, Corsair, London, 2019.
Reynolds, Barbara, *Dorothy L. Sayers: Her Life and Soul*, Hodder & Stoughton, London, 1993.
Sayers, Dorothy L., *Have His Carcase*, New English Library, London, 1974.
Sayers, Dorothy L., *The Letters of Dorothy L. Sayers*, ed. Barbara Reynolds, Hodder & Stoughton, London, 1995–2000.
Sayers, Dorothy L., *Gaudy Night*, Hodder & Stoughton, London, 2003.
Sayers, Dorothy L., *Busman's Honeymoon*, Hodder & Stoughton, London, 2016.

## PAUL GALLICO

Gallico, Paul, *Jennie*, Penguin Books, Harmondsworth, 1963.
Gallico, Paul, *The Silent Miaow*, Crown Publishers, New York, 1964.
Gallico, Paul, *Honorable Cat*, Greenwich House, New York, 1971.
Holtzman, Jerome, *The Gallico Adventure*, *New York*, vol. 7, no. 18, 1974.

## MURIEL SPARK

Spark, Muriel, *Robinson*, New Directions Books, New York, 1956.
Spark, Muriel, *A Far Cry from Kensington*, Constable, London, 1988.
Spark, Muriel, *All the Poems of Muriel Spark*, ed. Penelope Jardine, New Directions Books, New York, 2004.

Spark, Muriel, *The Informed Air: Essays*, ed. Penelope Jardine, New Directions Books, New York, 2014.
Stannard, Martin, *Muriel Spark: The Biography*, W.W. Norton, New York, 2010.
Taylor, Alan, *Appointment in Arezzo: A Friendship with Muriel Spark*, Polygon, Edinburgh, 2017.

DORIS LESSING

Klein, Carole, *Doris Lessing: A Biography*, Duckworth, London, 2000.
Lessing, Doris, *Particularly Cats and More Cats*, Michael Joseph, London, 1967.
Lessing, Doris, *The Old Age of El Magnifico*, Flamingo, London, 2000.

LYNLEY DODD

Dodd, Lynley, *Hairy Maclary from Donaldson's Dairy*, Penguin Books New Zealand, Auckland, 2014.
Dodd, Lynley, *Furry Tales: A Treasury of Cat Mischief*, Penguin Books New Zealand, Auckland, 2018.
Macdonald, Finlay, *The Life and Art of Lynley Dodd*, Penguin Books New Zealand, Auckland, 2013.

GENERAL

Eliot, T.S., *The Complete Poems and Plays*, Faber & Faber, London, 1969.
Guthrie, William, *The Life and Adventures of a Cat*, Willoughby Mynors, London, 1760.
Herriot, James, *James Herriot's Cat Stories*, Bantam Books, London, 1994.
Kalda, Sam, *Of Cats and Men: Profiles of History's Great Cat-Loving Artists, Writers, Thinkers and Statesmen*, Ten Speed Press, Berkeley CA, 2017.
Nastasi, Alison, *Writers and Their Cats*, Chronicle Books, San Francisco CA, 2018.
O'Mara, Lesley, *Cats' Miscellany*, Skyhorse, New York, 2011.
Smart, Christopher, *My Cat Jeoffry: A Poem*, Pelican Books, London, 1992.
Soden, Oliver, *Jeoffry: The Poet's Cat*, History Press, Cheltenham, 2020.
Méry, Fernand, *The Life, History and Magic of the Cat*, trans. Emma Street, Paul Hamlyn, London, 1967.
Robinson, Judith, and Scott Pack, *Literary Cats*, Bodleian Library Publishing, Oxford, 2022.
Walker-Meikle, Kathleen, *The Cat Book: Cats of Historical Dinstinction*, Old House Books, London, 2015.

# ACKNOWLEDGEMENTS

During the writing of this book I lost my beloved Maine Coon cat, Topaz. As I work on the revisions and write these acknowledgements the house seems empty without her glorious waving tail and her throaty purrs. I have been lucky enough to share my life with several cats – Abelard, Emily, Hamlet and Macbeth, Sheba, Clarence, Pearl and Topaz. I have loved them all and miss their affection and beauty.

Fortunately, my family shares my love of cats. My adored Dad, who died in 2023 and did not get to read this book, was always my biggest supporter and I miss him terribly. Three of my four siblings are 'owned' by cats, and I hope my brothers and sisters will enjoy this book. My husband Ian, my children Kenneth, Carrick and Elinor, and my son-in-law Craig have all given me warm support and encouragement. I hope that one day my adored granddaughters Arabella, Josephine and Florence will read my book and share their lives with cats.

Writing is an essentially solitary activity, so to discuss this book with good friends has been much-needed comfort. Gabrielle Black, Amanda Jones, Jennifer Kloester and Ruth

Wilson are truly purr-fect friends who enrich my life in so many ways. Cheryl Hill, who does so much to help me and is the biggest felinophile I know, has given invaluable technological help and encouragement. I could not do what I do without her! Rose Kirby, a very dear friend who died in 2024, shared my love of books and cats. I miss her hugely and think she would have enjoyed this book. My thanks also to Ruth Williamson, who helped and encouraged, and shares my love of cats. I would also like to thank Cathy Clay, who attended one of my lectures, noted a picture of an author with a pet, and suggested the topic of this book. You are a star, Cathy!

My grateful thanks to Dr Johnson scholar John Byrne, to Seona Ford (chair of the Dorothy L. Sayers Society), to sculptor John Doubleday, and to Dame Lynley Dodd for so generously sharing her personal history with cats.

It has been such a privilege to have this book published by Bodleian Library Publishing in Oxford and a real pleasure to work with editor Janet Phillips (and her beautiful cat Cleo). To all the team at the Bodleian – designers, illustrators, editors and marketers, and not forgetting artist's models Linus, Marbles and Hector – I give my warm thanks and appreciation.

*Great Writers and the Cats who Owned Them* was great fun to write, but books are nothing without readers. I hope that all who read it will enjoy encountering many different authors and discovering which puss made it into, or influenced, their writings.

*Susannah Fullerton*

# INDEX

Alcott, Louisa May, *Little Women*, 6
Andersen, Hans Christian, 82
Audebert, Nicolas, 23
Aung San Suu Kyi, 239
Austen, Jane, 157, 179, 183, 232

Bacon, Francis, 179
Barber, Francis, 16–17
Barber, Marjorie (Bar), 183
Barnett, Charis, 181
Barrymore, John, 100
Baudelaire, Charles, 4, 59, 244
Beaton, M.C., 21
Beckett, Samuel, *Human Wishes*, 21
Bedford, Grosvenor C., 49–50
Bellay, Joachim du, 104
Bentley, Richard, *Designs by Mr. R. Bentley for Six Poems by Mr. T. Gray*, 33
Bergh, Henry, 99
Bickley, Jon, 20
Blair, Cherie and Tony, 139
Blake, William, 34–5
 *The Tyger*, 201
Blume, Judy, 5
Blyton, Enid 232
Borges, Jorge Luis, 3

Boswell, James, 14–16, 21, 33
 *Life of Samuel Johnson*, 15–16
Bowles, Jane, 5
Bradbury, Ray, 3
Brecht, Bertolt, 5
Britten, Benjamin, 38
Brontë, Charlotte, 65
Brontë, Emily, *Wuthering Heights*, 7
Browning, Robert, 67
Buchan, John, *Huntingtower*, 178
Bukowski, Charles, 6
Burke, Edmund, 20
Burnford, Sheila, *The Incredible Journey*, 111–12
Burns, Robert, 111
Burroughs, William, 5
Burton, Dan, 230
Bryant, Doris, 149
Byrne, Muriel St Clare, 183
Byron, George Gordon, Lord, 23, 41

Campbell, Frede, 118, 120
Camus, Albert, 4
Carlingford, Lord, 68
Carroll, Lewis (Charles Lutwidge Dodgson), 86–7
 *Alice's Adventures in Wonderland*, 86–7, 141

Case, Frank, 100
Castro, Fidel, 155
Cave, Joseph, 171
Chamberlain, Neville, 132
Chandler, Raymond, 3
Chaucer, Geoffrey, *The Canterbury Tales*, 61
Chekhov, Anton, 4
Churchill, Clementine, 131, 133–4
Churchill, Mary, 131–2
Churchill, Sir Winston, 129–39
Clemens, Clara, 88
Clemens, Jane, 91
Clemens, Olivia, 88, 92
Clemens, Samuel *see* Twain, Mark
Clemens, Susy, 92
Clinton, Bill, 229–30
Clinton, Hillary, 229–30
Cocteau, Jean, 3
Coleridge, Hartley, 42, 50
Coleridge, Samuel Taylor, 40–41, 50
Coleridge, Sara, 40
Colette, Sidonie-Gabrielle, 102–10
  *Chéri*, 107
  *Claudine at School*, 106
  *Dialogues de Bêtes*, 106
  *La Chatte*, 108–10, 222
  *La Naissance du Jour*, 108
  *La Vagabonde*, 107
  *Le Blé en herbe*, 107
Collins, Wilkie, 82, 178
Colville, Sir John (Jock), 138
Congreve, Hubert, 71
Cook, Sir Roger, 19
Coolidge, Susan
  *Hodge the Cat*, 20
  *What Katy Did*, 20
Cowley, Joy, 27
Cust, Aleen, 75
Cust, Lady Mary Anne, 74–5
  *The Cat, Its History and Diseases*, 74

Dante Alighieri 173, 185
Darwin, Charles, *The Descent of Man*, 99
Darwin, Erasmus, 7
Dean, Dizzy, 193
Defoe, Daniel, 6, 10, 211
Dempsey, Jack, 193
Dexter, Stanley, 151
Dickens, Charles, 76–87
  *All the Year Round*, 84
  *Barnaby Rudge*, 80
  *Bleak House*, 79–80
  *David Copperfield*, 6
  *Dombey and Son*, 80
  *Oliver Twist*, 79
  *Our Mutual Friend*, 77–8
  *The Uncommercial Traveller*, 80
Dickens, Mary (Mamie), 80–83, 85
Dodd, Elizabeth, 236
Dodd, Dame Lynley, 231–42
  *Hairy Maclary* books, 231–2, 236, 237
  *Slinky Malinki* books, 237, 239
  *Titimus Trim* 236
Dodd, Matthew, 235
Dodd, Tony, 232, 235
Dotrice, Karen, 197
Doubleday, John, 182
Dumas, Alexandre, 54–9
  *Henri III and his Court*, 55
  *My Pets*, 55–6
Dumas, Alexandre, fils, 55, 59
  *The Lady of the Camellias*, 59
Dumas, Marie-Louise, 55–7
Dumas, General Thomas-Alexandre, 55

Eden, Anthony, 132
Eliot, T.S., 190–91
  *Four Quartets*, 190
  *Old Possum's Book of Practical Cats*, 4, 190–91
  *The Waste Land*, 190

Eliot, Valerie, 191
Elizabeth I, Empress of Russia, 139–40
Elizabeth I, Queen of England, 9, 98

Fleming, Oswald 'Mac', 175–7, 184
Flynn, Gillian, 4
Ford, Laura, 36
Forster, John, 82
Frame, Janet, 4
France, Anatole, 59
Frayling, Christopher, *Horace Walpole's Cat*, 36
Fricker, Mary 40

Gallico, Elaine, 193
Gallico, Paul, 192–202
  *Farewell to Sport*, 193
  *Honorable Cat*, 200–203
  *Jennie*, 192, 196–7
  *Manxmouse*, 194
  *Mrs. 'Arris Goes to Paris*, 194
  *The Adventures of Hiram Holiday*, 194
  *The Poseidon Adventure*, 194
  *The Silent Miaow*, 198–200
  *The Snow Goose*, 194
  *Thomasina*, 197
Gallico, Pauline, 194
Gallico, Virginia, 194
Garrick, David, 20
Gaskell, Elizabeth, 65
Gaulle, General Charles de, 104
Gauthier-Villars, Henri (Willy), 105–6
Gautier, Théophile, 4–5, 244
Geisel, Theodor, *see* Seuss, Dr
Gellhorn, Martha, *see under* Hemingway
Gibbon, Edward, 20
Gielgud, Val, 186
Glyn, Elinor, *Three Weeks* 3
Goldsmith, Oliver, 20

Gore, Al, 230
Goudeket, Maurice, 107
Granberry, Mabel, 164
Gray, Thomas, 25, 30, 34, 36
  *Elegy in a Country Churchyard*, 25
  *Ode on the Death of a Favourite Cat*, 31–6
Grimm, Jacob and Wilhelm, 45
Grose, Francis, *A Classical Dictionary of the Vulgar Tongue*, 85
Guthrie, William, *The Life and Adventures of a Cat*, 52–3

Hale, Kathleen, *Orlando the Marmalade Cat*, 35–6
Hampshire, Susan, 197
Hazlitt, William, 41
Heath, Edward, 5
Hemingway, Dr Clarence, 149
Hemingway, Ernest, 142–56
  *A Moveable Feast*, 150
  *Death in the Afternoon*, 153
  *Green Hills of Africa*, 153
  *For Whom the Bell Tolls*, 147
  *Islands in the Stream*, 147–8, 154, 156
  *The Garden of Eden*, 147
  *The Snows of Kilimanjaro*, 153
  *To Have and Have Not*, 153
Hemingway, Gregory, 142–3, 145
Hemingway, Hadley (née Richardson), 145, 150–51
Hemingway, John (Bumby), 150
Hemingway, Martha (née Gellhorn), 144–7
Hemingway, Mary (née Welsh), 147–9, 155–6
Hemingway, Patrick, 142–3, 145
Hemingway, Pauline (née Pfeiffer), 145, 151
Henry VIII, King of England, 9
Herriot, James, 3
Highsmith, Patricia, 215

Hill, Dr Nick, 60
Hogarth, Georgina, 84
Hugo, Victor, *Les Misérables*, 5
Hunt, Leigh, *The Cat by the Fire*, 20
Huxley, Aldous, 4, 7
Huxley, Thomas, 5

Innocent VIII, Pope, 9
Ivancich, Gianfranco, 154

Jackson, Peter, *Lord of the Rings*, 240
James, P.D., 182
Jardine, Penelope, 215–16
Jekyll, Gertrude, 5
Johnson, Elizabeth (Tetty), 13–14
Johnson, Dr Samuel, 9–21, 25–6, 33, 37, 178
  *Dictionary of the English Language*, 14, 16, 19, 20, 28
Jones, Bobby, 193
Jouvenel, Bertrand de, 107
Jouvenel, Colette de (Bel-Gazou), 110
Jouvenel, Henri de, 107
Joyce, James, 6

Kay-Shuttleworth, Lady, 65
King, Stephen, 3–4
Kipling, Josephine, 127
Kipling, Rudyard, 127–8
  *Just-So Stories*, 127
  *The Cat That Walked by Himself*, 127–8
Kurowsky, Agnes von, 150

Labay, Marie-Laure-Catherine, 55
Lamb, Charles, 41
Lamb, Mary, 41
Lambourne, Norah, 181, 183–4
Landor, Walter Savage, 40
Lapwood, Jack, 173
Le Guin, Ursula, 5
Lear, Edward, 62–75

*Illustrated Alphabet*, 63
*Illustrated Excursions in Italy*, 63
*Nonsense Songs and Stories*, 68
'The Owl and the Pussycat', 69–70
Leary, Katy, 90
Lee, General Robert E., 167
Leigh, Vivien, 170
Lessing, Doris, 219–230
  *On Cats*, 228
  *Particularly Cats*, 228
  *Rufus the Survivor*, 228
  *The Old Age of El Magnifico*, 227–8
Lewis, C.S., 179
Lincoln, Abraham, 167
Lincoln, Mary Todd, 167
Lloyd Webber, Andrew, 191
Longfellow, Henry Wadsworth, 82
Lorca, Federico García, 171
Loti, Pierre, 103

Macdonald, Chester, 120, 123
Macdonald, Rev. Ewan, 119–21, 123
Macdonald, Stuart, 120
McGoohan, Patrick, 197
Macmillan, George, 122–3
Macneill, Lucy Ann Woolner, 117–18
Mantel, Hilary, 38
Margaret, Princess, 171
Marlborough, John, Duke of, 130
Marquis, Don, 162
Marriott, John, 50
Marsh, John, 161–7, 170
Marsh, Ngaio, 5
Maugham, W. Somerset, 4
Maupassant, Guy de, 58–9
Menzies, Mel, 194
Méry, Dr Ferdinand, *The Life, History and Magic of the Cat*, 153
Mitchell, Eugene, 158, 161
Mitchell, Margaret, 158–71
  *Gone with the Wind*, 158–9, 162–3, 167–70

Mitchell, Maybelle, 158, 161
Mitchell, Stephens, 161
Montaigne, Michel de, 7
Montgomery, L.M., 113–26
  *Anne of Green Gables*, 114
  *Anne of the Island*, 123–4
  *Anne's House of Dreams*, 125
  *Emily of New Moon*, 124–5
  *Jane of Lantern Hill*, 122
  *Magic for Marigold*, 125
  *Mistress Pat*, 118
  *Pat of Silver Bush*, 118
  *The Blue Castle*, 123, 125
  *The Story Girl*, 125
Murakami, Haruki, 3
Murdoch, Dame Iris, 3

Nabokov, Vladimir, *Pale Fire* 21
Naipaul, V.S., 5
Newton, Sir Isaac, 60
Nicholson, Sir William, 133
Nightingale, Florence, 5
Nin, Anaïs, 4

Olivier, Laurence, 170, 225
Orléans, Louis-Philippe, duc d', 55–6

Parker, Dorothy, 100
Pepys, Samuel, 11
Petrarch, 22–3
Pindar, Peter, 85
Pirouet, Charles, 68
Plath, Sylvia, 5
Poe, Edgar Allan, 3
Poplawska, Rosa, 65–6
Potter, Beatrix, 6, 27, 141

Quadal, Martin Ferdinand, 35
Quincey, Thomas de, 41

Ravel, Maurice, *L'Enfant et les sortilèges*, 108

Reichenau Primer, 1
Reynolds, Barbara, 186
Reynolds, Sir Joshua, 20
Rousseau, Jean-Jacques, 16
Rowe, Dorothy, 183
Rowe, Nicholas, *Tamerlane*, 26
Rowling, J.K., 156–7, 194
  *Harry Potter* series, 156–7
Rubio, Mary Henley, 122
Ruskin, John, 41, 68

Saikia, Robin, *A Very Fine Cat Indeed*, 21
Sand, George, 7
Sayers, D.L., 173–89
  *A Cat's Christmas Carol*, 183
  *Busman's Honeymoon*, 187
  *Clouds of Witness*, 188
  *Gaudy Night*, 178
  *Murder Must Advertise*, 188
  *Pussydise Lost*, 188
  'The Cyprian Cat', 188
  *The Documents in the Case*, 180
Sayers, John Anthony, 185, 189
Scott, Sir Walter, 41
Seuss, Dr (Theodor Geisel), 27, 217, 232, 236
  *The Cat in the Hat*, 217–18
Shaw, George Bernard, 5
Shelley, Percy Bysshe, 41
Sitwell, Dame Edith, 3, 246
Skargon, Yvonne, *Lily and Hodge and Dr Johnson*, 21
Smart, Anna, 37
Smart, Christopher, *Jubilate Agno*, 37–8
Smith, Alexander McCall, 5, 38
Soden, Oliver, *Jeoffry: The Poet's Cat*, 38
Southey, Caroline, 51–2
Southey, Charles, 43–4, 48–9
Southey, Edith, 40, 51
Southey, Edith 48

Southey, Robert, 39–52
  *Life of Nelson*, 40
  *Memoirs of the Cats of Greta Hall*, 42
  *The Three Bears*, 39
Spark, Dame Muriel, 204–16
  *A Far Cry from Kensington*, 208
  *Curriculum Vitae*, 213
  *Robinson*, 211–12
  *The Comforters*, 205
  *The Informed Air*, 211
  *The Prime of Miss Jean Brodie*, 212–13
Spark, Robin, 204
Stannard, Martin, 206
Starmer, Sir Keir, 139
Stevenson, Robert Louis, *Dr Jekyll and Mr Hyde*, 233
Stewart, Al, 73
Stockdale, Percival, 16, 18
  'An Elegy on the Death of Dr Johnson's Favourite Cat', 18–19
Stowe, Harriet Beecher, 5
Strachey, Sir Edward, 69
Strahan, William, 14
Sutton, Eve, 235–6

Taine, Hippolyte, 7
Tasso, Torquato, 184
Tennyson, Alfred Lord, 67
  *Maud*, 167
Tennyson, Emily, 63
Thackeray, William Makepeace, 4, 85
Thompson, Hunter S., 5–6
Thrale, Hester, 18
Thurman, Judith, 109
Twain, Mark (Samuel Clemens), 4, 88–99
  *A Cat Tale*, 95
  *A Cat-Loving Family*, 95
  *A Dog's Tale*, 99
  *A Horse's Tale*, 99
  *Autobiography*, 93–4, 99
  *Dick Baker's Cat*, 97
  *Pudd'nhead Wilson*, 91
  *Rambling Notes of an Idle Excursion*, 98
  *Roughing It*, 97–8
  *The Adventures of Huckleberry Finn*, 96
  *The Adventures of Tom Sawyer*, 95–6
  *The Innocents Abroad*, 98
  *The Mysterious Stranger*, 97
  *The Refuge of the Derelicts*, 96
Twichell, Rev. Joe, 98

Uezzell, Adelaide, 205–6
Upshaw, Berrien (Red), 161

Verdi, Giuseppe, 59
Villareal, René, 147, 149, 154
Voltaire, *Zaïre* 27

Walker, Alice, 3
Walpole, Horace, 24–38
  *The Castle of Otranto*, 30
  *The Funeral of the Lioness*, 34
Walpole, Sir Robert, 24, 27
Weir, Harrison, *Our Cats and All About Them*, 83
Wells, H.G., 4
Williams, Tennessee, 4
Wolf-Ferrari, Ermanno, *The School for Fathers*, 172
Wolsey, Cardinal Thomas, 129
Woolf, Virginia, 5–6
Wordsworth, Dorothy, 41
Wordsworth, William, 41
Wright, John M.F., 60
Wuest, Brigitte, 240

Zola, Émile, 103